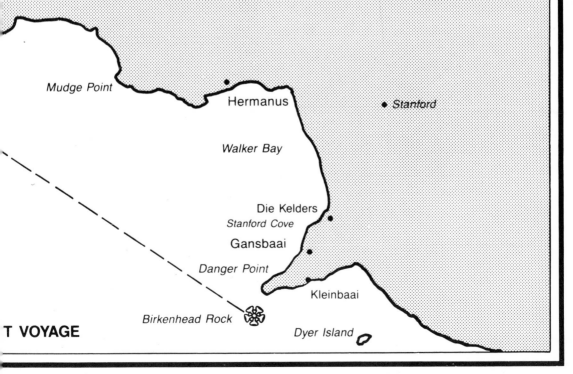

Caledon ●

Mudge Point

● Hermanus

● Stanford

Walker Bay

Die Kelders
Stanford Cove

Gansbaai

Danger Point

Kleinbaai

Birkenhead Rock

Dyer Island

T VOYAGE

Salvage
of the
Birkenhead

Salvage
of the
Birkenhead

Allan Kayle

SOUTHERN
BOOK PUBLISHERS

ISBN 1 86812 260 3

First edition, first impression 1990

Published by
Southern Book Publishers (Pty) Ltd
PO Box 548, Bergvlei 2012
Johannesburg

Set in 11 on 13 pt Chelmsford
by Unifoto, Cape Town
Printed and bound by CTP Book Printers, Cape
BK1028

Contents

For my wife Jean Anne, with love.

Acknowledgements

I had a dream. I had friends with courage. From nothing grew a team, a machine and an incredible project. Outsiders laughed and mocked us; they told us we were mad and it was impossible. They tried to tempt us back into the places for sheep, the safe, featureless places where unfulfilled hearts bleat at each other. But we were like eagles and lions, determined and strong and daring. We will never be sheep and we salvaged the wreck of HMS *Birkenhead*.

To the men of the project:

Italo Martinengo, Charlie Shapiro, Mike Keulemans, Malcolm Ferguson, Erik Lombard, André Hartman, Nick Bartlett, Ken de Goede, Alan Holton, Pierre Joubert, Albert Botha, Konrad Stutterheim, Paul van der Merwe and André Steenberg; and to Captain Ernie Fitzgerald and the men of the *Reunion*, and Captain Clive Gibson and the men of the *Causeway Adventurer*,

I offer you my joy and my pride in your strength, your spirit and your power.

To those who believed in us and proved it:

Pero Alfirevich, Captain Ockert Grapow, Dr Chris Loedolff and Jalmar Rudner,

I offer you my everlasting gratitude and friendship.

To those who helped us:

Safmarine, Pentow Marine, Alfirevich Transport, Liquid Air, Techmar Engineering, Michael and Aubrey Diamond, Haggi Rand, Tony and Martin Nassif, Anglo American and First National Bank Ltd,

I offer my thanks and heartfelt appreciation.

To·the regimental museums of those who died with the *Birkenhead*:

The Queen's Royal Surrey Regiment, the Royal Warwickshire Regiment, the Suffolk Regiment, the Royal Green Jackets Regiment, the Worcestershire and Sherwood Foresters Regiment, the Black Watch, the Royal Highland Fusiliers, the Argyll and Sutherland Highlanders, and the Royal Lancers,

I thank you for your great interest, encouragement and enthusiastic support.

My gratitude to those who helped with the research:

Robert Crichton Durno, Barbara Horrocks, David Bevan, Miss E. Talbot Rice of the National Army Museum, Mrs Diana Wall of the Africana Museum, Geoff Davies, the National Maritime Museum, the Johannesburg Public Library, the State Library in Pretoria, the South African Library in Cape Town, and Cammell Laird Shipbuilders.

To Ione Rudner, who edited my first manuscript and showed me a new road, my deepest affection and appreciation.

To Charlie Shapiro, who made his drawings and photographs available for this book, and to Paul van der Merwe who provided his photographs, my very sincere thanks and respect for your talent.

To all the women who lived without their men for so many months every diving season, thank you for your patience.

Prologue

It was the mid-1830s and a time of great technological development. Sail and wood, the ancient and traditional means of sea transport, were being challenged. The glorious days of sail, the billowing clippers, the elegant schooners and the tall-masted windjammers were faced with the advent of a noisy, grimy and bustling newcomer – the steamer. Shipyards with dwindling stacks of scarce timber – teak, oak and cedar – focussed on a clanging banging material – iron. Hand in hand, iron and steam entered the industrial scene and with their servants, fire and water, began conquering the civilised world.

Steam-driven iron-hulled commercial vessels appeared, with paddles splashing through the water on both sides or propellers thrusting from behind. Desirous of lucrative government business, shipbuilders submitted designs for iron-hulled warships to the British Admiralty. All were rejected. The Admiralty was adamant that an iron-hulled warship would sink, it would be too difficult to repair, barnacles would foul its

John Laird, the builder of the Birkenhead

hull, its durability would be inferior to wood, and compass errors would occur due to the large amount of iron present.

Shipbuilders such as John Laird in Birkenhead, England, disagreed. Determined to prove his point, and without any behest from the Admiralty, Laird in 1836 began building a 55-m iron-hulled side-paddle steamer rigged with sails and armed as a frigate. The Admiralty refused to consider it. Mexico was at war with Texas and, following the British rebuff, Laird sold the vessel to the Mexican government who named her the *Guadeloupe* and took her to war. Fighting under Commander Charleswood, an ex-officer of the Royal Navy, the *Guadeloupe* was invincible. Laird's *Nemesis* followed, and her success between 1840 and 1843 in surviving gales, hull damage, and then hectic service as a gunboat in the China War, eventually persuaded the new Board of the Admiralty to begin purchasing iron warships.

Shipbuilders rushed in with their plans. Among them was Laird with the designs for his frigate *Vulcan*. Almost 64 m long and displacing 1 918 tons, the *Vulcan* was typical of the transition from wind to steam power. Rigged as a brigantine, she had a foremast and a fore and aft mainmast. A tall funnel, leaning slightly backward and stabilised by guy ropes, stood between the foremast and the fore mainmast. Her figurehead was an effigy of Vulcan, the god of fire and patron of metalworkers, holding a thunderbolt in one hand and a hammer in the other. She had two steam-driven 6-m diameter side-paddles sited amidships with a beam of 11,3 m between them.

Vulcan on the prow; a picture of the original plan

The composite body of the *Vulcan* reflected the period of change in ship construction from wood to iron. Her hull was of iron plates rivetted together, while her decks and paddle boxes were wooden. The iron plate below the water-line was 15,8 mm thick, overlapping with double rows of alternating rivets. Above the water-line the plate was 14,3 mm thick, joined flush with a single row of rivets to an internal iron strap. Iron bulkheads dividing the ship into several watertight compartments were installed. As a frigate, she was to carry two 96-pounder swivel cannons, one fore and one aft, and four 68-pounder deck cannons, two on each side.

The plans were approved with modifications. Her paddles were ordered to be moved several feet forward, despite Laird's assertion that this would make the vessel trim by the head unless carefully stowed. Her name was changed. A propeller-driven iron-hulled frigate also called *Vulcan* had been ordered (together with three others – *Simoom, Greenock* and *Megaera*), and Laird's *Vulcan* was renamed the *Birkenhead*. Her large swivel cannons were scrapped and it was decided that she would be converted into a troopship.

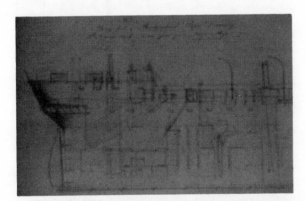

Stern plan of the vessel, as modified for a troopship

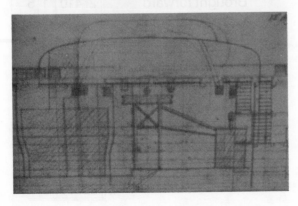

Paddle wheel, engine and boiler plan section

COSTING OF HMS *BIRKENHEAD*

From the original balance sheet as kindly supplied by Cammell-Laird in Birkenhead.

No. 51	Birkenhead Frigate			
Hull				
Ironwork	7320 5 0			
Time	10092 2 0	17412 7 0		
Tradesmen Painting & Sidelights		93 1 5	17505 8 5	
Woodwork				
Ironwork	173 15 6			
Time	368 15 0	542 10 6		
Timber	3948 19 8			
Sundry materials	30 17 8			
Carpenters' wages	1873 8 0			
Joiners	1152 3 6	7005 8 10		
Tradesmen		1134 19 5	8682 18 9	
Cabins				
Ironwork	127 0 6			
Time	19 0 0	146 0 6		
Timber	302 12 4			
Sundry materials	23 7 1			
Joiners' time	612 5 3	938 4 8		
Tradesmen		137 9 1	1121 14 3	
	Carried forward	£	27410 1 5	

No. 51	Birkenhead			
	Brought forward		27410 1 5	
Outfit				
Ironwork	25 4 8			
Time	24 18 0	50 2 8		
Tradesmen		57 1 11	107 4 7	
Sundries				
Sundry expenses		206 17 7		
Commission		1505 0		
Incidental expenses		2912 0 0	4623 17 7	
		£	32141 3 7	

4

Toward the end of December 1845 the *Birkenhead* was launched, the Marchioness of Westminister naming the vessel. The enthusiastic reporter of the *Illustrated London News*, Saturday, 24 January 1846, wrote: 'She is in fact all that can be desired by the most critical judges in naval architecture, sharpe at both extremities, yet with that fulness and rotundity of bottom and bearings which which will enable her to do her work well, "Blow high, or blow low".' [*Sic*]

Her engines had to be installed and she was towed to her berth. Two single-pistoned engines with a collective 350 horse power made by Messrs. George Forrester and Co. were mounted and then coupled to her side-paddles.

Politics again intervened. The Whig opposition seized on the iron ship issue in an attack on the Tory government. Leading the storm was Sir Charles Napier, angry at losing a large sum of money in the company owning the iron-hulled *Aaron Manby*; a ship he himself had captained to Le Havre and Paris with great enthusiasm. Following Napier an immense amount of resistance to iron vessels reoccurred in the Admiralty.

In 1844 a series of tests to determine the effects of cannon shot on iron hulls had been conducted in great secrecy at Woolwich Arsenal. A 32-pounder gun fired solid shot with varying propellant charges against different qualities and thicknesses of iron from 12,7 mm to 38 mm. Some plates were backed with several thicknesses of wood and others with kamptulicon (a mixture of rubber and cork). The results were reported in 1846. They showed that a shot at normal velocity made a clean easily-plugged hole. A nearly spent shot made a jagged hole, more difficult to plug. A large number of splinters, deadly over a considerable radius, came from both the plate and the shot which invariably broke up. These splinters could be eliminated by backing the iron plate with 356 mm of wood or kamptulicon.

In 1846 the *Lizard* and the *Harpy*, two gunboats in service up the Parana River in Uruguay were heavily shelled by shot, grapeshot and musket balls. The *Lizard* lost four men with four wounded while the *Harpy* suffered one wounded. Splinters of metal flying from the hulls were blamed and the fact that the casualties were relatively light for the harsh punishment taken was ignored.

The Opposition seized upon the splinter issue.

Under pressure from Parliament, the Admiralty decided to test the effects of shot on iron hulls once again. A controlled test, such as the one at Woolwich Arsenal, was not performed. Instead, an iron tender *Ruby* was chosen as target, ignoring the fact that her iron plates, only 3 mm thick to begin with, were nearly rusted through. From a range of

400 m, the training ship *Excellent* bombarded the *Ruby* with her 8-inch and 32-pounder guns. Most of the shot passed right through the shabby *Ruby*, smashing the pathetic little tender to pieces.

By the end of 1846 official hope for the future of iron ships was lost. The Admiralty decided to cut its losses and cancelled most of its orders for iron frigates, retaining only those for the *Simoom*, the *Megaera* and the *Vulcan*. In addition, their engine power was reduced to save fuel and increase available space. Wooden ships once again became the order of the day for the Royal Navy and remained so for another decade until the emergence of armoured frigates.

For nearly eighteen months after her engines had been fitted, the *Birkenhead*'s work was confined to the waters around Britain. In September 1846 the *Great Britain*, Brunel's splendid iron-hulled passenger ship and then the largest ship in the world, ran aground in Dundrum Bay on the coast of County Down. She had been bound for New York from her berth in Liverpool. For eleven months she lay high and dry on the beach of the Irish coast.

Pocket watch belonging to Cornet R.S. Bond, photograph provided by Major R.M. Collins

The innovative salvor James Bremner was given the job to refloat her after numerous attempts to do so had failed. He drove twenty massive logs into the sand on either side of the vessel. Ropes from the bottom of the *Great Britain* were passed over grooves in the top of each log and attached to twenty suspended boxes of sand, each weighing fifty tons. As the boxes dropped, so the ship would rise. He added huge levers; long thick poles were rammed under the hull and anything heavy was fixed to their outer ends – anchors, rocks and even iron lifeboats filled with sand. With each high tide she rose a little higher and tons of stones were poured down slides into the space that formed to prevent her from dropping again. Eventually her two holes were exposed. A team of Portsmouth boilermakers patched these. The boxes were then emptied of their sand and fixed to the *Great Britain* to increase her buoyancy.

HMS *Birkenhead* under Captain A.H. Ingram and HMS *Scourge* were summoned. Together the steamers towed the giant passenger ship 6 m further out to sea. On 27 August 1847 the *Birkenhead* towed the *Great Britain* another 145 m into deeper water, where she anchored. After being stranded for nearly a year, *Great Britain*'s engines and boilers were unusable. Her hull still leaked. The *Birkenhead* towed her to Belfast for hull repair, and then across the Irish sea to the yards in Liverpool.

A few months later work began to convert the *Birkenhead* into a troopship. Then the Admiralty, weary of spending money on their 'monstrous iron vessels', called a halt. She was laid to at her moorings in Portsmouth, where she languished for nearly two years. In late 1850 work was recommenced, her bulkheads penetrated for personnel access and easy troop transfer, and a poop deck and forecastle fitted. In 1851 the troopship *Birkenhead* under her new commander, Robert Salmond, began carrying troops to the Channel Islands and Lisbon, then later that year to the Cape Colony for the Eighth Frontier War.

FEBRUARY 1852						
SUN	MON	TUE	WED	THU	FRI	SAT
1	2	3	4	5	6	7
8	9	10	11	12	13	14
15	16	17	18	19	20	21
22	23	24	25	■	27	28
29						

A painting of the Birkenhead under full sail and steam by Peter Bilas

Troopship Birkenhead *in Table Bay 1852. T.W. Bowler. Permission: William Fehr Collection, Cape Town*

Wreck of Her Majesty's Steam Frigate Birkenhead. *Wintergerst. Permission from Africana Museum*

Women and children on the poop. T. Hemy. Permission from Africana Museum

Proposed Birkenhead Memorial at Danger Point. P.R. Davis. Permission from Africana Museum

A Tradition is Born

On 23 February 1852 the *Birkenhead* anchored in Simon's Bay. She had been battered by a terrible Atlantic storm after leaving Cork in Ireland the previous month, losing three women in premature labour and a fourth who died of tuberculosis. Taking on fresh water, provisions, wine, 350 tons of coal, horses and straw, the *Birkenhead* steamed out of Simon's Bay at about 18h00 on the evening of 25 February. She was bound for Algoa Bay to land the drafts of the 12th, 74th and 91st regiments, and then proceed to the Buffalo River to land the remainder – the 12th Lancers, the 2nd, 6th, 45th and 73rd Foot, the 43rd Light Infantry, and a detachment of the 60th Rifles. It was a perfect night, the sky clear and the sea flat and calm. On deck, Captain Edward Wright, officer in charge of the 91st Foot, was chatting to the naval officer on watch, Second Master R.D. Speer. It was 21h30.

'We have passed the lighthouse,' said Speer, pointing portside to a light on land.

'Surely that is not the Agulhas lighthouse,' replied Captain Wright. 'If so, it must have been moved nearer Cape Point than it was when I was here five years ago.' He gazed across the flat, starlit sea at the light, compared it to the numerous fires burning on the distant mountainside, shrugged and said, 'They must have built another lighthouse since I was here in 1847.' He stretched, yawned, and bidding Speer goodnight, retired to his cabin.

At 22h00 Able Seaman John Haynes took the wheel. Second Master Speer was waiting. 'Steer south-south-east, half east,' he ordered. He seemed restless, continually checking the compass reading and gazing out for the first sight of the Agulhas lighthouse (still over 90 km away). Leaving the poop, he stopped at the port paddle box and stared ashore. He returned and indicated the compass bearing. 'Make sure that you do not steer eastward of the course,' he instructed. 'Keep a quarter of a point to windward of it.'

Steadily the *Birkenhead* continued on her passage. Midnight passed and it was 26 February 1852. Second Master Davies took over as officer of the watch. Almost everyone was sound asleep in their quarters, lulled by the churning of the side-paddles and the rhythmic deep thumping of the two steam-driven piston engines. Only a few groups of men at their posts attended the paddle steamer. Able Seaman Francis Holditch and Seaman Thomas Cuffin had taken the helm from the grateful Haynes, weary and anxious to get to his bunk. As the time was called at 01h00, Ordinary Seaman Thomas Daley took the look-out on the starboard bow, and John Butcher the port. Leadsman at the after part of the paddle box and a prisoner was Abel Stone. At the call he hurled the lead weight for a depth sounding. There was no slackening of the attached calibrated cord. The water was too deep to sound, and travelling at 8,5 knots made an accurate sounding very difficult. Down in the cavernous engine-room, Assistant Engineer Kitchingham was engineer of the watch. Perspiring freely and feeding the boiler fires with brick-like chunks of coal were stokers John Ashbolt and William Chase. It was just an ordinary night, the men inured to the demands of the lonely small-hour vigil. Colour Sergeant John Drake of the Royal Marines stepped up on to the forecastle.

Towards 02h00 the *Birkenhead* approached Danger Point, about 180 km from Cape Town. Her black-painted iron hull merged with the surrounding darkness, only the white of her paddle box covers and her lifeboats glimmering in the night. High above the wooden deck her three masts stood with furled sails, and between the foremast and the mainmast smoke poured from her tall funnel.

She was minutes away from her end. Abel Stone took a sounding. Twelve fathoms of line sped through his fingers then the line went slack. 'Sounding twelve fathoms!' he called.

Daley and Butcher on the bow scanned the water ahead. It glowed sleekly calm in the starlight. Sergeant Drake looked at the shore. It lay about four points on the port bow.

With her paddle wheels churning at full ahead the ship rammed an uncharted rock, ripping open the forward lower troopdeck. Iron plating tore jaggedly inwards and a wall of icy cold sea water hurtled into the troops' sleeping quarters. Suspended shoulder to shoulder in their hammocks, hundreds of soldiers were suddenly slammed against the iron sides and bulkheads of the deck under a torrential inrush of water.

High up on the forecastle, Sergeant Drake and seamen Daley and Butcher were hurled against the railings as the *Birkenhead* came to a sudden crashing stop. Captain Salmond, awoken by the terrible shock, ran from his quarters on the port main deck and rushed to the wheel. Rapidly assessing the situation, he commanded, 'Stop engines!'

The order echoed in the engine-room. Mr Kitchingham ran to the starting gear and halted the engines. At that moment Benjamin Barber, the assistant engineer, came rushing in from his quarters.

'I have just stopped the engines!' shouted Kitchingham. Chief Engineer W. Whyham stormed in. 'Open the safety valves of all three boilers!' he yelled. Barber ran to do this. Charles Renwick, the chief assistant engineer, arrived dressed only in his shirt. Water was pouring into the engine room from the main deck through the door over the starboard cylinder. Wading and gasping through the flood, Renwick reached and closed the door.

Men were streaming on to the open deck from below. Captain Salmond and Mr Davies, still at the poop, were joined by Captain Wright.

'How was the light bearing when you last saw it?' Salmond demanded of Davies. Davies answered, then as the captain turned away to rap out a stream of orders, Davies shakily commented to Wright, 'It *was* odd where that light was.' (Captain Wright was later to report that he believed that the light was not a lighthouse, as Davies thought, but a fire lit at Cape Mudge to serve as a signal fire for the fishing boats that go out from that point.)

Lieutenant John Francis Girardot of the 43rd Foot and Ensign G.A. Lucas of the 73rd Regiment arrived at the wheel. They had been on watch duty. Their uniforms contrasted sharply with the rumpled and scanty clothing of the men on deck. Lieutenant-Colonel Seton, now also at the poop, took command of the soldiers. Summoning all his officers about him, he impressed upon them the need to preserve order and silence among the men. His voice cut through the night. 'Captain Wright!'

'Sir!'

'Take and have executed whatever order the commander may give!'

Instantly obeying, Wright turned to Captain Salmond and received the command to put 60 men on to the chain pumps on the lower afterdeck.

'Lieutenant Girardot, attend to this,' ordered Wright. 'Have the men told off in three reliefs.'

Meanwhile, Master's Assistant Richard Richards, also savagely awakened in his hammock in the fore cockpit, ran on deck in his shirt. He looked down the fore hatchway and saw that the cockpit was half-full of water and filling very rapidly. The screams of injured and drowning men echoed up from the darkness. Rushing aft, he heard the captain's order to man the pumps. He returned to the after cockpit and with the ship's carpenter and the purser's steward, shipped the pump handles, then returned on deck. Captain Salmond was issuing directive after directive.

11

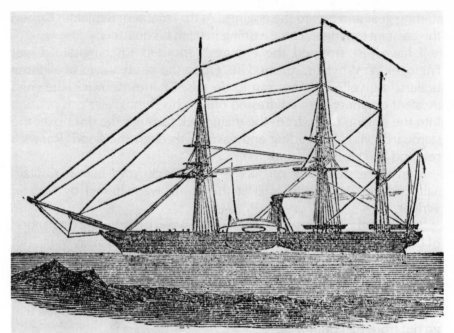

THE "BIRKENHEAD" NEARING THE SUNKEN ROCK.

STRIKING THE ROCK.

BREAKING.

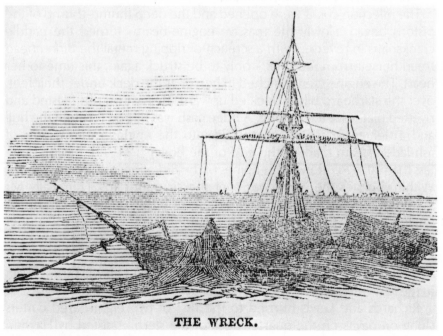

THE WRECK.

From The London News, *10 April 1852, with permission from the Africana Museum*

'Soundings, Mr Stone!' 'Seven fathoms alongside, two fathoms under the bows, and eleven by the stern, captain!'

'Sergeant Drake! Carry my orders to Master Brodie. Instruct him to drop the small bower anchor, get out the port paddle box boat, and get the women and children into the boats.'

He addressed Captain Wright. 'Attend Mr Brodie on the bridge and enquire what assistance he requires to get the paddle box boats out.'

Hurrying to Master Brodie (second in command of the ship), Wright was told to put thirty men on each paddle box tackle to get the boats off. Having ordered this, he returned to the commander on the poop. The iron forward hatches, dividing the flooded bows from the rest of the vessel, had been closed. By now, about ten minutes had passed since impact.

Robert Salmond gazed at the submerging bows impaled and anchored on the rock. The *Birkenhead* was swinging and grinding and grating in the long onshore swell. 'She will start breaking up before the boats are away,' he murmured to himself. He decided to back the ship off the rock.

Down in the engine-room, Mr Whyham, his engineers and the stokers were awaiting the captain's orders.

'Turn astern!' came the command.

The injection cocks were opened and the deep thump-thump of the pistons began. Slowly the massive engine-beams turned the paddle crankshafts in reverse. With a screech of ripping metal the *Birkenhead* freed herself from the rock – only to be struck again, this time to her heart. The engine crew watched in horror as the deck under their feet, over the starboard bilge, buckled upward. Heavy iron ribs twisted and rivetted plates started tearing. A huge gash was ripped through the hull and a deluge of sea water poured into the engine-room. Gouts of ash-laden steam marked the end of the boiler fires and, having done less than 20 revolutions, the engines of the *Birkenhead* stopped forever. Within minutes the water was over the air pump lids. Frantically Mr Whyham reported to the captain, then shouted, 'All hands out of the engine room!' Clambering up the ladders they reached the upper deck.

The captain's orders were flying.

'Mr Richards, lower the quarter boats! Mr Lewis, you will be coxswain in the first cutter! Mr Archbold, fire the rockets and both blue lights!'

Richards and Lewis hurried to the first of two eight-oared cutters slung on davits on the quarter-deck of the stern. Assisted by Haynes, the helmsman of the first watch, and Daley, the look-out on the starboard bow, the cutter was lowered. Lewis, Haynes and Daley leapt aboard and waited alongside the troopship. Richards then made for the starboard paddle box boat falls.

Captain Salmond had come from a proud line of seafarers, dating back to the late 1500s. His four brothers as well as his father had all died on active service at sea. He had two sons, one of whom had also perished at sea while still in his teens. The other was to become the grandfather of Lieutenant-Colonel G.P. Gofton-Salmond O.B.E. of the 45th Regiment of Foot, now known as the Sherwood Foresters, with whom I was to have the privilege of correspondence.

Robert Salmond from a family portrait, used with permission of Brenda Gofton-Salmond.

The long line of breeding was now in full evidence. He addressed Lieutenant-Colonel Seton: 'Have your men gather on the poop deck, so as to ease the weight on the forepart of the ship.' Speedily this was accomplished with remarkable calm and discipline. The milling hundreds of confused, young and inexperienced soldiers drew courage from the proud and calm bearing of Alexander Seton and obeyed immediately.

The seven women and thirteen children aboard were now huddled together under the poop awning. Quartered deep in the middle and lower decks of the stern, they had waited in uncomprehending terror following the impact and the ensuing commotion above. Dressed only in their nightclothes and holding hastily grasped shawls, they had been escorted through the dark passageways via the deserted officers' mess and then up the ladder-ways to the upper deck.

Captain Salmond turned to Cornet Ralph Sheldon-Bond of the 12th Lancers, the officer in charge of the horses. 'Pitch the horses out of the port gangway!'

To Mr G.W.S. Hire, the clerk of the *Birkenhead*, he said, 'Get the books ready to go in the boat.' Seeing the fear in Hire's eyes, he added more softly, 'I do not think there is any immediate danger.'

Calling for Mr Richards, he commanded, 'Get the women and children into the second cutter and save them!'

As the second cutter was lowered it took on a wash of sea water and was almost swamped alongside the *Birkenhead*. Richards clambered down and, with Able Seaman George Till as coxswain, assisted the women and children as they were passed into the boat. From the gangway some soldiers jumped aboard and, with a total complement of thirty-five persons, they manned the oars, stopping about 100 m off to watch the end.

Gunner Archbold's rockets and lights lit up the night sky – to reveal a terrible scenario. Her bows deep in the sea and her engine-room flooded, the *Birkenhead* was writhing in her death throes. At the forepart of the vessel, Able Stone, the prisoner who had sounded the depth, was assisting in lowering into the water the gig to which he had been assigned. The two cutters were waiting in the sea nearby. At the

Birkenhead *sinking; a painting by R. Sheldon-Bond of the 12th Lancers who survived the wrecking, used with permission of the Sherwood Foresters Museum*

starboard paddle box the ship's crew assisted by thirty soldiers were preparing to lower the boat. On the opposite side, an equal number of soldiers together with Sergeant Drake, Gunner Archbold and Mr Brodie were struggling to free the canted port paddle box boat. A rusted pin defied them.

Lined up on the poop deck, hundreds of soldiers stood barefoot, their eyes fixed on Alexander Seton and his officers standing before them. Some were dressed only in their nightclothes, others in what smatterings of uniform they had managed to grab. Many were injured and naked, their garments torn from them during their clawing escape from the flooded troop quarters. Amidships, men were labouring to free the pinnace, the largest boat on the *Birkenhead*, lying directly in front of the funnel.

Alerted by the commotion, sharks began swimming around the ship, vague sleek shapes gliding through the water, their dorsal fins barely visible in the darkness.

A terrible groan of yielding iron came from the bows. Just as the gig rowed free, the *Birkenhead* tore behind the foremast. The bows cocked up, thrusting the bowsprit high in the air before sinking, while the middle of the ship dipped deeper into the sea. The stern tilted high in the air sending the tall crenellated funnel crashing down. It smashed the central pinnace and hit the starboard paddle box, crushing the men clustered there before tumbling over the side.

Caught off-balance by the lurching deck, men fell into the sea. Water surged over the paddle boxes. Brodie, Drake, Archbold and scores of soldiers were washed overboard. Spars, debris, pieces of furniture and bits of wreckage from the sunken bows were floating in the water.

'Save Brodie!' yelled Captain Salmond from the poop. Fighting his way to the surface, Archbold grabbed and held on to a portion of wreckage before swimming to a truss of hay where he found Master Brodie, injured and clutching the flimsy bale.

A second growl of ripping metal began. A rent appeared just in front of the paddle boxes, lashed down and astern, and the *Birkenhead* broke in half. Great gouts of air gushed to the surface as the entire foresection disappeared under the sea. Dropping from its steep tilt to an even keel, the stern began sinking rapidly. Down in the lower deck, the scores of soldiers manning the chain pumps in waterlogged darkness drowned.

Captain Salmond, Mr Speer and Mr Hire were still at the wheel, the last now clutching the logbook and manifest of the *Birkenhead*. Behind them on the poop were Dr W. Culhane, assistant surgeon, and Dr R.

Bowen, second staff surgeon. The massed young soldiers and officers stood and waited without cry or murmur.

'All those who can swim, jump overboard and make for the boats!' called Captain Salmond. Upon hearing this command, Dr Bowen lowered himself into the water and swam to the first cutter.

On a calm sea, under a starry sky and without an enemy in sight, the great naval tradition of 'women and children first' was born. Standing in the poop tails, Captain Edward Wright and Lieutenant John Francis Girardot cried out to the men, 'Do not go overboard to the boats! You will swamp them and the women and the children!'

The ranks stood still. The deck gave a final convulsive surge, throwing Captain Salmond into the water. Every officer and the hundreds of scantily clad, untrained and untried men stood fast and went down with the poop.

Down and down dropped the flooded stern, the tall mainmast sliding vertically, silently and almost gracefully into the sea until, with an unsensed crash, the keel hit the ocean bed. The top of the mainmast and the main topsail yard protruded above the water like a giant crucifix marking the site of a watery grave.

Only twenty minutes after striking, the *Birkenhead* was gone. The water was full of struggling men, crying and shouting for help.

Part of the forecastle deck was floating about 20 m from where the poop went down. Swimming for it, Captain Salmond was struck heavily on the head by a piece of poop wreckage and disappeared, never to rise again. Nearby, and witnessing the death of his captain in the night-black water, was Sergeant Drake. Also nearby, choking and splashing in the night, was young Cornet Rolt of the 12th Lancers. Wide-eyed and terrified, he pleaded, 'Please save me!' The powerful marine swam to Rolt and helped him on to a portion of floating debris. He then made for the protruding mainmast on to which Hire the clerk, his books gone, and dozens of men were clinging. The raft supporting Rolt broke in a sudden surging swell and the lancer vanished.

At the extreme end of the stern of the *Birkenhead* a dinghy had been mounted on davits. The little boat was lost before ever being used. As the poop sank, Assistant Engineer Barber, his legs dangling in the water, held on to the empty fall. The weight of frantic soldiers clutching at him forced him to let go. He grabbed at the main rigging, only to find himself being drawn under water as it slid down into the sea. Clawing and kicking his way to the surface, he held on to a fragment of wreckage.

Captain Wright, together with five others, had managed to climb on to the floating fore sponson. As the wood drifted, they pulled up nine or ten more hapless men, including Archbold (who had left his bale of hay as it broke up), Barber and Lacey James, a boatswain's mate. Mr Brodie had drowned.

Dr Culhane swam for the gig and was helped aboard. Assistant Engineer Renwick was also swimming. He had decided to make for the shore. Seeing two boats to his left, he approached the first and called for help. Mr Richards' voice answered, 'We are full, go to the other boat.'

As he approached, Renwick suddenly sank as a young soldier grabbed him and pulled him down. Struggling free, he rose and was hauled into the gig semi-conscious. He recovered to find Dr Culhane and six or seven others in the boat.

Cornet Sheldon-Bond was one of the few to have had a Mackintosh life preserver. He inflated it in the water. Around him men were clinging desperately to floating debris, thrashing in the water before drowning, or shrieking as they were taken by sharks.

The boats were full and no more men could be rescued from the water. The first cutter held thirty-six soldiers and sailors, the second thirty-five people, including the women and children, and the gig nine men. Only eighty of an initial complement of 638 had found a place in the boats. As the boats pulled away, the wails of those still struggling to reach them echoed over the swells.

It was now nearly 03h00 and the sea was quiet. More than forty-five men were clinging to the projecting mainmast. Unable to swim, terrified to leave their pathetic refuge, they elected to wait for help. Others held on to bits of debris and began drifting towards land. Some lashed themselves to these pitiful rafts, slumping exhaustedly on to them as the current bore them from the scene.

The long night wore on. Several men on the mast had gone, dead of exhaustion, cold and injury. In the early morning, as mist rolled over the beaches and rocks, soldiers began reaching the shore through the thick seaweed and breakers.

Cornet Sheldon-Bond, supported by his Mackintosh life preserver, swam the two kilometres to shore. Exhausted, he struggled through the seaweed at dawn and followed a track along the beach. There, head hanging and standing spent near the surf, was his horse! Leading the animal from the water, he returned to the site of his landing. Nine men on a driftwood raft were frantically trying to row ashore with makeshift paddles. Others were holding on to bits of wood and kicking and splashing for safety. Bond shouted and waved from his rock, indicating the passage he had taken through the kelp. They landed at 07h00. Lieutenant Girardot was one of them.

Wearily they made their way inland. The thick bush and thorny scrub tore at their bodies and bare feet as they trudged. Sixteen kilometres later, exhausted, famished and bleeding, they met Captain Smales, an ex-7th Dragoon Guard at his farm 'Klyne River' near Stanford.

Captain Wright and the men with him on the sponson drifted into Walker Bay and reached the thick seaweed in the early afternoon. After fighting their way through the kelp, they too began to march inland in search of aid. Many of the men were naked and nearly all were without shoes. To maintain morale under woeful conditions, Captain Wright made them sing, and ragged strains of 'The Bay of Biscay O' rose from the little band of British soldiers. At 15h00 they met a wagon-driver who directed them to a fisherman's hut at Stanford's Cove. They reached it at sunset, but there was nothing to eat. As night fell again, Captain Wright left his men, walked another 12 km through the darkness to a farmhouse and sent back provisions for the soldiers. Next morning wagons and food were dispatched and the men transferred to Captain Smales's farm.

It was Friday 27 February. Bond and Girardot had returned to the rocks and beaches at Danger Point where they met Captain Wright who had begun the search for survivors.

Both paddle box boats had been washed overboard when the *Birkenhead* broke. The port boat was keel uppermost and, sprawled on it, seven or eight men had floated to land. The other was upright and almost full of water. When it drifted ashore, one of the ship's quartermasters crawled out and collapsed on the beach. Remaining in the boat lay seven dead men, all naked. The quartermaster was fully dressed.

Other rafts were coming ashore carrying dead soldiers and sailors lashed to them. Bodies washed up, some horribly mutilated by sharks.

For three days, Wright and James Jeffreys, the purser's steward on the *Birkenhead*, combed the dunes and rocks over a distance of 32 km up and down the coast, staying in a hut each night. They found two survivors. The crew of a whaling-boat that had been working at Dyer Island helped in searching the kelp. Rowing up and down outside the treacherous seaweed, they found another two men who had spent 38 hours in the water. On Sunday afternoon the search was called off.

All the surviving soldiers were now at Smales's farm and had been clothed from his farm store. The Civil Commissioner of Caledon, Mr Mackay, and a party of men under Jan de Villiers, the local field-cornet, accompanied Captain Wright to bury the bodies on the beaches and collect the things that had washed up on shore.

Five horses, including Bond's, had managed the long swim to shore and were put into Mackay's custody for later transferral.

The two cutters and the gig had closed in the night, keeping close together as the screams and moans of dying men faded and disappeared.

They rowed north-east into Walker Bay, the roar and crash of the breakers becoming louder and louder, then fading as they passed Danger Point. Richards, commanding the second cutter with the women and children, approached the shore. The surf was running high. Almost swamped as they neared the breakers, and rowing desperately to escape their power, he yelled to the other boats to stay back. Reunited, they began rowing towards Cape Hangklip, searching for a place to land.

At dawn, a schooner's sail appeared about 8 km off. They decided to try and reach her. Pulling at the oars, the trio of boats rowed after the schooner for two hours, but made little progress in nearing her. As the cutter with the women and children fell behind, Dr Culhane in the gig suggested that the eight strongest men man the gig and chase the ship. Crossing over from the gig, Assistant Engineer Renwick took command of the first cutter, and watched as the gig set off in pursuit.

A wind had sprung up and as hard as the gig's crew rowed, the schooner steadily gained and eventually disappeared. The cutters, now far behind, were out of sight too. Alone and uncertain as to what would be best to do, the gig with the ship's surgeon and the eight men with him made for shore. Rowing east into Walker Bay they landed during mid-afternoon at a small cove that they called Port D'Urban. The fishing folk at Herries Bay swarmed to their assistance. Borrowing a horse from a resident, Michiel Henn, Dr Culhane rode to Cape Town and nearly 24 hours later, the exhausted surgeon related the news of the disaster.

Henn, a shrewd fisherman, retained the gig as security for his horse. The horse was never returned and Henn kept the gig. He named it *Nellie*, and for many years *Nellie* was to give faithful service as a fishing boat, before sinking in the lagoon at Hermanus.

The cutters had been separated during the initial chase after the schooner. Further out to sea, Renwick was obliged to pull before the swells in a stiff south-easter to avoid being swamped. At 10h00 Captain Thomas Ramsden on the schooner *Lioness* spotted them. Tacking, he reached the cutter at midday, took aboard Renwick and the thirty-six exhausted men, hauled up the cutter, and heard the shocking news of the disaster. A search began for the two other boats.

On the other cutter the presence of the twenty women and children hampered the oarsmen and, being able to pull only six oars, Richards' boat had again started for land. In the distance they could see the top of the mainmast of the *Birkenhead* projecting at the wreck site, but could not distinguish any men. Flying a sail made from a woman's shawl spread on a boat-hook, they were spotted by the *Lioness* which reached them just before 13h00. The women, children and soldiers were taken aboard, where Captain Ramsden and his wife hurried to provide clothing, food, drink and comfort.

The search for the gig proved fruitless, as it was already skirting the shore. Turning about, the *Lioness* made for the wreck. At 14h00 she reached the site. The men aboard gazed in horror at the 45 parched, spent and nearly naked men clinging to the rigging and waving and croaking hoarsely at their salvation. The two *Birkenhead* cutters, now aboard the *Lioness*, were again lowered. Richards and Renwick took charge of these and, rowing to the mast, took off the men and helped them board the schooner. A total of 116 people saved were now on the *Lioness*.

Dr Culhane's news aroused immediate action. Commodore Wyvill on board HMS *Castor* in Simon's Bay, ordered the steamer *Rhada-manthus* to make for the site to search for survivors. On the night of 27 February, the *Rhadamanthus* under Commander B.H. Bunce met with

EXTREME PERIL OF THE " CASTOR'S" LAUNCH, SENT TO SURVEY THE BIRKENHEAD ROCK.

From The London News, *16 October 1862, with permission from the Africana Museum*

the *Lioness* and her survivors on board. As speed was essential and the wind had died, the *Rhadamanthus* towed the schooner to Simon's Bay then returned to the scene of the wreck. No more survivors were found in the sea. Only the desolate mast with its furled remnants of sail was left.

Captain Edward Wright's group was located at Smales's farm near Stanford, while some were staying in a house belonging to 'Granny' Moore, the wife of a Mr John Moore. Boarding the *Rhadamanthus* at Stanford's Cove, they left the area and reached Cape Town on 1 March.

Of the 638 persons on board the *Birkenhead*, 445 had died.

Discovering a Legend

Although I had heard of the *Birkenhead*, I really knew nothing about it and was intrigued to read in *The World Atlas of Treasure* by Derek Wilson that she had been carrying £3 000 000 of army payroll to the Cape and, though the *Birkenhead* had been located, no one had yet raised the coin. I there and then decided that I would initiate a salvage expedition and the decision changed my life.

I began to read about the *Birkenhead* in libraries in Johannesburg and Pretoria and became fascinated by the saga and heroism of the *Birkenhead* soldiers. My family was saturated by my continued prattle and enthusiasm for the wreck. Again and again I regaled them with the story of the disaster and each new fact that emerged from my research was recounted *ad nauseam*. One day when I visited my in-laws Robert and Junae Durno a friend of the family arrived. Geoff Davies, a lover of history, motor-cycles and weapons, pressed a book into my hands. It was *Drums of the Birkenhead* by David Bevan, for which I had been searching for months. I was ecstatic with delight. As I devoured that book, it became obvious to me that a salvage effort would be fraught with problems. This was a British war wreck, the soldiers had died under conditions of revered heroism, and the tragedy was the origin of the great naval tradition of 'women and children first'. I became deeply concerned about the moral and ethical implications of such a salvage. The regiments represented on the *Birkenhead* were among the cream of British military pride. They were the 2nd Foot, now known as the Queen's Royal Surrey Regiment; the 6th Foot, now known as the Royal Regiment of Fusiliers; the 12th Foot, now the Suffolk Regiment; the 43rd Light Infantry, now the Royal Green Jackets; the 45th Foot, now the Worcestershire and Sherwood Foresters Regiment; the 73rd Foot, now the Black Watch; the 74th Foot, now the Royal Highland Fusiliers; the 91st Foot, now the Argyll and Sutherland Highlanders; and the 12th Lancers, now known as the 9th/12th Royal Lancers.

I decided to contact each of them, explaining my idea of a salvage and requesting their views on the moral implications. Once again

ABOVE: *The Birkenhead Rock*

LEFT: *Remnants at the bows*

BELOW: *Alan Holton on scuba. Coloured sponges and coral on the rock*

Anchor fluke emerging from the sand

Dead-eye in sand

A brass porthole, heavily disguised in conglomerate, lies near a leg of the triangulation ring

Geoff Davies came to the rescue. 'Why not contact the National Army Museum in London?' he asked. 'There is a lady there by the name of Miss E. Talbot Rice who is very helpful and most knowledgeable.' My letter to Miss Talbot Rice requesting details of the regiments was promptly answered.

On 12 June 1983 I wrote to each of the regiments. Daily I waited for the postman, rushing out to see whether I had received a reply. On 26 June I had my first answer – from the Argyll and Sutherland Highlanders regimental headquarters. Not only were there no objections, but I received their 'best wishes for a successful venture'. As the next few days passed, letter after letter arrived. Every regiment gave me the go-ahead and their encouragement! My excitement knew no bounds when I received a letter from Lieutenant-Colonel G.P. Gofton-Salmond O.B.E. of the Sherwood Foresters, the great-grandson of Captain Robert Salmond, the master of the *Birkenhead* who had died with her.

It was now time to obtain permission to perform the salvage. In South Africa, the National Monuments Council issues permits for the salvage of wrecks older than 50 years. This responsibility was vested in the NMC in terms of legislation passed in 1981 to protect the undersea heritage from indiscriminate looting. South African waters are rich in sunken wrecks, several dating back to the 1500s. The advent of scuba gear during the 1940s gave hundreds of divers easy and relatively inexpensive access to many of these wrecks. Much of the material has consequently been removed and the *Birkenhead* is no exception. During the 1950s, Tromp van Diggelen obtained permission to salvage the *Birkenhead*. This was a salvage permit only: an archaeological or historical assessment was not a prerequisite. A permit from the NMC implies cultural and archaeological care, and it is now a criminal offence to remove anything from a historical wreck without NMC approval.

During the months of July and August 1983, correspondence, queries and answers flowed between the NMC and me, until, day of days, on 7 August 1983 I held in my hands the sole permit to salvage the *Birkenhead*. Naturally, this called for a celebration – with a reverently opened bottle of fine champagne.

It was time to plan the techniques that would be used to do the work. So much had to be done, so much had to be arranged. It was to take two and a half years of further toil, investigation, and research before the salvage could begin.

In 1981, one of my close friends, Italo Martinengo, and I had trained as amateur scuba divers. Diving became our food and drink. We were happy only when the air we breathed was compressed in a bottle. Within a few months, however, we began to get restless. We needed something to do, something that would challenge our newly acquired diving skills.

The concept of a diving bell arose, a machine that would allow us to descend in a closed, protected environment to the bottom of the sea, and then be lifted back to the surface. A team was needed to man the system and share the expense of its construction. Italo approached Alan Holton, a scuba diver with many years of experience. At least two more were required. Alan then discussed the project with two of his friends, Pierre Joubert and Ken de Goede. During the winter of 1982 the five of us met for the first time at Ken's home.

We needed two chambers. One would be a mobile diving bell, lowered by a surface crane to the seabed and the other a fixed surface decompression chamber on to which the bell and its pressurised occupants would lock after being lifted from the sea. The chambers were designed and work commenced. Italo had a large engineering works and was superbly competent to handle all the elaborate computerised machinery. We decided that all the lathe and milling work required for the pressure-proof doors and windows would be done under the guidance and expertise of Italo. These would then be delivered to the pressure vessel factory for welding into the shells. Every single piece of steel we handled had to be certified and stamped by the appropriate authorities. We learnt to grind, cut and shape back-breakingly heavy lumps of steel. We broke expensive drills, cutters and a variety of machines during our progress, but progress we did. Basic lathe work and milling were learnt. We shivered on cold winter nights and weekends as these were the only times we had available, all of us having to work for a living and pay for the hungry maw of our growing baby. Summer came and we sweated where before we had shivered. A routine was established and the work on the diving system became a normal part of our lives. Free weekends were a thing of the past and free nights a luxury. Every week we visited our developing shells, watching in fascination as the enormous automated welding machine sealed the seams of the vessels, and with trepidation as the portholes were cut into the bell.

We all sat down together to discuss where we were and where we were going. At this time it had become obvious that we were in for much more than we had initially bargained for, and we had to determine just how elaborate we were going to make the system. As our knowledge and experience had grown, so had our hopes and demands on the diving chambers. We decided to go for broke and build a full saturation system, a diving system with full life-support capabilities which could keep divers under strictly controlled conditions and under pressure indefinitely. Temperature, gas concentrations, humidity and so on would be strictly monitored. Toilet and washing facilities, bunks for sleeping and resting, food, water and clothing – all these had to be incorporated.

Steel bunks to support four divers were built and fitted. Highly sophisticated and reliable valving was imported from America, the same type used by NASA in their space programme. Elaborate alloy tubes were brought in from England and special gauges ordered from Germany. Our commitment both financially and in determination was now complete. We had decided to go for broke and we were. A bank account under our registered name, Depth Recovery Unit (Pty) Limited was opened and overdraft facilities were arranged.

The Depth Recovery Unit team. From left to right: Allan Kayle, Alan Holton, Ken de Goede, Pierre Joubert and Italo Martinengo

During spring 1984 we were given marching orders by the owners of the barn-like room we had been using for our work. We had three weeks to move our 10-ton yellow foetus and no incubator to put it in. Rental on a closed space large enough to accommodate us was beyond our available finances which were scarcely enough to purchase the equipment we needed.

There is a benevolent spirit who smiles on maniacal aspirations: within a week of receiving notice to move we had a new home, rent free, in a larger and better situation.

In Johannesburg is a firm belonging to Pero Alfirevich, who arrived in South Africa as a refugee from Yugoslavia. Recognising a kindred entrepreneurial spirit, Pero cleared a section of his workshop for us and welcomed us on our arrival with a buffet lunch! As we rolled our chambers through the entrance on to the site, champagne and home-made biscuits arrived. Some debts can never be repaid – what is the price of friendship and an open heart? We were to continue our work in this most happy of homes for more than a year before our toils were done and the long road to the coast was begun.

Seeking for More Knowledge

Our permit, while granting us permission to undertake a maritime archaeological salvage and excavation of the *Birkenhead*, had several very explicit conditions and restrictions. We had to co-operate with the South African Cultural History Museum and the Department of Archaeology at the University of Cape Town. Up to half of the artefacts salvaged could be claimed by the museum at no cost. Inspectors from these institutions and from the NMC had to be allowed access to the wreck site and storage areas. All data and collections had to be made available to the Cultural History Museum until recorded and studied. Progress reports on the salvage had to be made to the NMC every three months. No material from the wreck could be exported without the permission of the NMC. To protect us from 'pirates', the site was provisionally proclaimed a national monument, covering an area within a radius of 500 m of Birkenhead Rock.

My letters to both the Cultural History Museum and the Professor of Archaeology at UCT elicited gratifying interest, especially in my request for guidance in techniques of preservation and restoration. A time of intensive research began. I spent days in the darkest depths of libraries, seeking information from the newspapers of the time. As the majority of these were on microfiche, my world became a flickering blur of negatives and spinning film.

Immediately following the disaster, newspapers in the Cape Colony and later those overseas gave enormous coverage to the tragedy. The heroism of those soldiers in sacrificing themselves to save the women and children caught the imagination of the world. In subsequent weeks, the tenor of the news changed as goods, clothing and blankets were washed ashore. It was decided to sell the *Birkenhead* and the items that had come ashore.

A notice appeared in the *Supplement to the Government Gazette and Trade List* on 25 March 1852, one month almost to the day after the *Birkenhead* sank:

WRECK OF H.M. STEAMER
"B I R K E N H E A D"
WRECKED OFF DANGER POINT
Near the farm of Sir Robt. Stanford.

ON MONDAY MORNING next, the 29th instant, will be sold, by
Public Auction, on the Beach of DANGER POINT the above Vessel,
as she lies in the Sea, with RIGGING, SPARS, YARDS, &c., &c.,
STORES AND PROVISIONS, and whatever may be on Board.

ALSO
WEARING APPAREL

Consisting of Naval and Military Clothes, Shirts, Shoes, Stockings,
and whatever may have been washed on Shore from the above Wreck.

R.J. JONES, Auctioneer

Two days before the sale, on Saturday 27 March 1852, the following
three items appeared in the *Graham's Town Journal*:

Lieut. Girard, 43rd, arrived at King Williams Town today with the
remainder of the ill-fated *Birkenhead* troops. There are several inci-
dents of a most heart-rending character. Several of the poor fellows
were torn off the yards and planks by sharks, which selected all the
men without clothes. It is said that Major Seton had a life preserver
on, and foolishly secured 300 sovereigns round his neck, and strange
to say, his pistols. It is thought that the weight of these kept his head
under water, and thus he perished.

The officer of the Lancers who was saved from the *Birkenhead*, had
great luck in saving 150 sovereigns, and on reaching the shore found
both his horses had landed. We hear that the *Birkenhead* had watertight compartments, but in such a rusty state that the slides could not
be closed, and that all her boat tackle was rotten – so much for the
boasted trim of our naval armament.

Wreck of the *Birkenhead* – Information has been forwarded to us,
that 49 bodies have washed up from the wreck, and buried. The body
of Dr Laing was recognized having a gold watch and £18 in money
upon it. 47 packages of officers' clothing have also been washed up,
and are now lying at Capt. Smales.

It is expected that the wreck will soon break up. – *Cape Monitor.*

Only five officers survived the wreck – Captain Wright, 91st regiment; Lieutenant Girardot (whose name always seemed to be spelt incorrectly), 43rd Foot; Lieutenant Lucas, 73rd Regiment; Cornet Bond (the officer of the Lancers referred to in the item), 12th Lancers; and Staff Surgeon Bowen.

Ten days later the *South African Commercial Advertiser* of Wednesday 7 April 1852 printed this article:

> Up to the last accounts 91 bodies, together with several mangled remains, have been washed up from this ill-fated vessel. The wreck has been sold for 135 pounds, and the various articles that have been washed up, consisting chiefly of blankets and clothing, for 100 pounds. All traces of her above water have entirely disappeared.

The *Birkenhead* had gone but the search had just begun.

On Saturday 10 April 1852 the *Graham's Town Journal* reported:

> A cutter was despatched a few days ago by the Commodore from Simon's Bay, for the purpose of ascertaining by observation the exact position of the spot where the *Birkenhead* was wrecked. Mr Munn one of the assistants at the Observatory, proceeded in this cutter, in company with a naval officer and some six or seven seamen. We understand that they experienced some very severe weather, and were nearly lost in consequence of the cutter being in danger of being swamped. They with difficulty reached Table Bay yesterday morning, much exhausted from their exposure and fatigue. They were unable to accomplish the object for which they were despatched.

Not everybody wanted to return to sea. The *Graham's Town Journal* of Saturday 17 April 1852 put out this notice:

> King William's Town, 11 April 1852.
>
> Description of a Deserter of the 2nd (or Queen's) Regiment of Foot, who deserted from Cape Town on the 6th March 1852:
>
> WILLIAM BABB, (one of the survivors of the wrecked H.M. steamer *Birkenhead*) 5 feet 6½ inches high, light complexion, light brown hair,

grey eyes; by trade labourer; had on at the time of desertion plaid waistcoat, and grey trousers.

RICHARD STACK Esquire
Comdg Detachment 2nd (or Queen's) Ft.

The first major book on the *Birkenhead* was *A deathless story* by A.C. Addison and W.H. Matthews, published in 1906 in London by Hutchison and Co. On page 117 one reads:

The wreck itself, with all that it contained, was sold by public auction by the agents of the Admiralty at the Cape, acting in conjunction with the Officers of the Customs there or other Colonial authorities, and early in 1854 it was announced that a Mr H. Adams and a band of divers were engaged on the wreck at Danger Point.

The search for the 250 000 gold sovereigns she was reputed to have carried was on. In 1854 diving equipment was in its infancy and the dive was a very deep and dangerous one for the facilities used. (It was to take another 87 years before scuba was invented.) Adams did apparently manage to recover Lieutenant-Colonel Seton's writing desk, some silver engraved with the family crest, and some of his personal belongings.

The newspapers of the following eight years were scanned for further reports. On 7 June 1862 *The Cape Argus* reported:

THE WRECKED STEAMER BIRKENHEAD – It is understood that a company in England has recently purchased this steamer, as she now lies submerged near Cape L'Agulhas, for 2 780 pounds: and that a number of artizans may shortly be expected to arrive for the purpose, if possible, of raising her. It will be in the recollection of many that at the time of the melancholy disaster – about ten years ago – she went down with a considerable amount in specie on board, and was then sold by public auction for 50 pounds to two gentlemen, who have since transferred their interest in her to the above company.

Anything that this company may have found went unreported, but the search for the gold was to go on.

Ensign Lucas of the 73rd Regiment, who survived the shipwreck and later became resident magistrate in Natal, formed the first 'Birkenhead

Grant's condenser stropped for lifting

The triangulation ring under water. A nylon tape is attached to the end of the pivot-rod

Digging down into the sand with the airlift

ABOVE: *Getting ready to lift the unit at the docks*

RIGHT: *Two helpers begin stripping Italo after his dive, while a second pair assist Malcolm over the ladder*

BELOW: *A pensive moment on the Reunion. From left to right: Alwyn Kuhn (a photographer), Captain Ernie Fitzgerald, Erik Lombard*

Erik Lombard getting ready to dive off the Reunion

Crane mounted on the Causeway Adventurer

Water smashing over the stern as the Adventurer pitches

Rifle trigger guard, side plate and musket balls

Syndicate' in 1893, where investors could 'make a comparative fortune at a trifling outlay' by speculating £15.

In the book *A deathless story* the tale continues:

At the end of 1893 (writes the nephew of Colonel Seton) a certain Mr Bandmann at the Cape got leave from the Government to dive at the wreck of the *Birkenhead* in search of some supposed treasure on board, said to amount to 240 000 pounds in gold, for payment of the troops etc, at the seat of war. My late uncle, David Seton, hearing of this was apprehensive lest, if any of his brother's effects not affected by sea water, such as silver spoons, dirk, shoe buckles, etc, were recovered they might be sold or exhibited as relics of the wreck. He therefore got a memo. sent to Lord Loch, the then Governor at the Cape, by which he was to instruct Mr Bandmann that in the event of any articles belonging to officers or men on board the *Birkenhead* being recovered and identified, they were to be handed over to their relatives. The minute went on to say that, as regards any treasure that may be recovered, one-third was to be handed over to the authorities at the Cape, and Bandmann could keep the remaining two-thirds.

As one diver tried and failed to find the reputed sunken gold, another soon appeared to take his place.

On 2 December 1898 the *Cape Times* reported:

A Mr. J.W.L. Baumann is "treasure seeking" at the wreck, and that divers had declared that they had seen safes screwed to the ship, but were unable to remove them without better appliances than they had.

For over a quarter of a century the *Birkenhead* seems to have been left alone. Then in 1935, Rossi, a salvage expert with the Sorima Company of Genoa (which salvaged the gold on the *Egypt* near Brest, and copper off the *Cariboo* near East London) attempted diving the site. The weather and the sea turned on the salvors and their salvage efforts proved a failure.

Another 23 years passed. In 1957, Tromp van Diggelen, the South African body-builder, strong man, big game hunter, and racing driver, initiated the next salvage project to find the gold. Van Diggelen had a burning ambition to salvage the *Birkenhead*, locate its bell and return it to England. Together with a number of Cape Town businessmen a second *'Birkenhead* Syndicate' was formed to find the gold. A faded photocopy of the original document was found at the Johannesburg reference library. Unfortunately undated, the prospectus reads:

PROSPECTUS
"BIRKENHEAD" SYNDICATE.

Telegrams:- "HERAKLES"   SOUTH WEST HOUSE
Telephone 2-8826   GREENMARKET SQUARE
P O Box 2398   CAPE TOWN
CAPE TOWN

Despite unfavourable weather, enough material has already been salvaged from the wreck of the "BIRKENHEAD" to prove that the Syndicate's method of free-diving is the only correct one for the type of work that is here demanded. With the coming of better weather conditions during the Summer, and owing to exact plans of the sunken vessel having been supplied by the Maritime Museum in London, work can be continued with great confidence and plans are being made for extensive recoveries. Enough copper has already been found to bring in a considerable amount when it is brought up to the surface; anchors, and other valuable relics, have been "buoyed" to be salvaged later.

The vessel contained much military equipment as well as a great variety of articles of value. The most efficient methods will be employed to "comb" every part of the wreck and much gold coinage should be recovered "loose" as many men had their pay, in gold sovereigns, on their persons when they were suddenly drowned below decks. Hundreds of sea-chests will also be explored for valuables and golden coins. Every corpse that floated ashore carried sovereigns in a belt or in pockets of clothing; over 600 soldiers and sailors had received pay on the day before the catastrophe.

When the gold in the safes is found then each Syndicate share of £1 will be worth over £100. There is no reason to think that the gold is NOT on the wreck. During the past 80 years, divers have been sent to the wreck on three occasions by the Navy. Cumbersome diving suits prevented any success. The last officer to leave the sinking ship was Ensign Lucas, a young man who was a great favourite amongst all personnel on board. Lucas later became Chief Magistrate of Durban. While still Resident Magistrate, Captain Lucas, as he was then known, initiated a "Birkenhead" Syndicate, "The Concessionaire having the sole rights to remove the £300 000, sunken treasure". These rights are

---

now held by Tromp van Diggelen, the organizer of this Syndicate. In the first Syndicate's Prospectus these words appear: *"Capt. Lucas (Resident Magistrate, Durban) survivor, states that there was more than £300 000 on the vessel when she floundered".* In the Cape Times of the 2nd December, 1898 is a paragraph stating that two divers had actually reached the wreck and found two safes attached to the side of the vessel; owing to inadequate equipment they were unable to salve the safes and never again made an attempt.

Each investor in the present Syndicate will receive (free of charge) from Tromp van Diggelen, shares to the value of his investment in the "Birkenhead" Syndicate, in the new Salvage Company which will be inaugurated by the experts from Holland at the end of this year. There is also a certainty of a good, general recovery of material and relics of value, and a very good chance of gold worth over £1 000 000 being salvaged. Members of the "Birkenhead" Syndicate will receive 20% of all recoveries. The Syndicate is limited to £1 500. Cheques should be made payable to the "Birkenhead" Syndicate. Any amounts received after the necessary capital of £1 500 has been attained, will be returned forthwith and no shares will be available when the gold has once been found.

(Signed) Tromp van Diggelen
ORGANIZER

In Hermanus there used to be a hotel called The Birkenhead, named after the shipwreck. It had a pub and it is not difficult to imagine what the commonest topic of conversation in that pub would be. Sitting at the bar one day, Van Diggelen was discussing the wreck with a friend of his. Quietly having a drink nearby was Nicholas Dekker who over-heard their conversation, became involved in it in the way men do in pubs, and promptly joined the project. Nicholas Dekker was to be the diver on the *Birkenhead* project.

From a twin-screw launch, the *Penta*, Dekker dived on the *Birkenhead* from the summer of 1957 to April 1958. It was not an easy business. His twin eight-litre scuba cylinders had to be taken to Cape Town nearly 200 km away for each refill of air, as a local compressor was not available. The weather was very unreliable and weeks would go by in which Dekker would be unable to dive. He worked alone and limited his dive to twenty minutes at a time as no decompression facilities were available in case of a problem. His air supply was just about exhausted by that time anyway. The launch had only one anchor and 'a half-baked crew' and most of the time he was terrified that the anchor would drift or part, leaving him stranded at the rock to make the long swim for land.

He began by swimming down the pinnacle where he found a bow anchor dropped so many years ago. Following the anchor chain, the bows, engine and, further away, the paddle wheels were found. Portholes, stanchions, ventilators, spars, copper and brass items, and bronze blocks with wooden sheaves still containing their ropes were recovered.

The stern of the *Birkenhead* was missing. The entire aft half of the troopship was gone. Between and beyond the paddle wheels, which had been sited amidships, a bare sand-filled area extended northwards. Bounded by rock on the starboard side and empty sand to port, this space should have held the stern. The poor visibility prevented a proper search of the area. Because Dekker was diving alone such a search would have been a very risky procedure in any event. The stern had remained afloat longer than the rest of the wreck and could have settled further away or been carried far from the rock by the currents.

The military officers and the women and children had all been quartered in the stern. The gold, if aboard, would have been kept close to the officers. The stern and the gold seemed lost forever.

Tromp van Diggelen's quest was the sixth recorded salvage attempt on the *Birkenhead*, and its failure to find the gold signalled the end of the second '*Birkenhead* syndicate'.

Getting Closer

It was time for me to digest all the research that had been accumulated.

Following the disaster, a court-martial was held aboard HMS *Victory*, lying at Portsmouth harbour. Accused were the 59 surviving crew members of HMS *Birkenhead*. No officers had survived to face charges for the loss of the vessel. As their statements were recorded, it was confirmed that the *Birkenhead* had broken into three sections. The first break had occurred just behind the foremast and the second just in front of the paddle boxes, leaving the stern as the last and largest fragment.

Although all the men were acquitted, the question why the *Birkenhead* had passed so close to shore while rounding Danger Point remained unanswered. One possibility that has been suggested is that the watch mistook lights ashore for those of Cape Agulhas (the southerly tip of Africa). This is unlikely, however. The survivors' reports clearly describe the restlessness of Master Speer and his preoccupation with searching the shore for the first sight of the lighthouse. While chatting to a local fisherman at Gansbaai, I was given another possible explanation. The local people talk of a race to break the record to Algoa Bay. Perhaps too fine a cut was taken on the corner around Danger Point? The truth will never be known.

Several facts were certain. The *Birkenhead* had broken into at least three sections: the bows, the engine-room section and the stern. As the last break had occurred through the engine-room, the stern section would be the largest fragment and would consist of the entire aft half of the vessel. We knew that the officers and passengers were quartered in the stern and that the stern had not been located. At least six reported salvage attempts on the *Birkenhead* had taken place. Salvors are notoriously reticent about reporting and proclaiming their finds so we had no idea as to what had already been removed. Between 1958 and 1983 literally hundreds of scuba divers had dived at the wreck and taken artefacts from her.

Several questions arose. Why did the *Birkenhead* break up so badly and quickly? Could we find the stern? Was the gold loaded aboard the

Birkenhead? If so, was it in the stern? Had it been removed by previous salvors in secret?

A new perspective had to be gained. We had undertaken to perform a scientific salvage of the *Birkenhead,* with due regard for the historical, cultural, and archaeological aspects of the wreck. We could do nothing whatsoever about any previous salvage work and had to accept and work with the wreck as she now lay. The only viable approach was a thorough and methodical exploration of the whole area. We would use all the technology available to us to locate and identify every section of the *Birkenhead,* including the missing stern.

If gold were aboard and it had not already been removed, we would find it. It was simply a matter of time and hard work. There were certainly a number of pointers to its existence.

Lieutenant-Colonel Seton was reported to have had 300 sovereigns upon him when he drowned, although these could have been personal monies and the report was only hearsay.

Cornet Bond 'had great luck in saving 150 sovereigns'.

The wreck had been bought for £2 780 in 1862. This was a huge sum for those days. Moreover, there was only a small chance of success with the primitive diving expertise available. To this day, the Admiralty has denied knowledge of any gold aboard the *Birkenhead.* Why then, would anyone spend such a sum in 1862?

Ensign Lucas had formed the first '*Birkenhead* Syndicate' in 1893. Why would a surviving officer of the wreck initiate such a syndicate if the quest was a fruitless one?

In his book *The unfortunate ship,* published by George G. Harrup and Co. in 1960, J. Lennox Kerr states: 'Another survivor, Corporal O'Neill, was also sure that the troopship carried treasure, and wrote, "I believe there was a lot of treasure on board the *Birkenhead* when she floundered. The military chest was on board for the troops – so we were led to understand. I think it is true, because for some time afterwards we were paid in Mexican dollars."'

Much more definite proof was obtained by poring through the original hand-written court-martial records at the Public Records Office in England. One of the reports reads as follows:

CM 7th May 1852

Report on Courtmartial (continued)

Mr Richard Bevan Richards
master's assistant was
again recalled –

By the Judge Advocate

Q. Was there any leadsman in the chains previous to the ship sinking?
A. Yes. *Stone*, one of the prisoners.
Q. Did you hear him give any soundings?
A. Yes, but I did not take any particular notice.
Q. Where were you when the *Birkenhead* struck?
A. I was below.
Q. When did the ship strike?
A. A little before two o'clock.
Q. When were you sensible to this fact?
A. When the impact took place, I looked at the cabin clock, it may have been a minute after she struck.
Q. Was she under sail or steam or both?
A. She was under steam alone.
Q. Do you know what the *Birkenhead* was carrying?
A. Yes. Troops, Government stores and specie.
Q. Do you know how many troops?
A. Not exactly without looking at the records.
Q. Do you know what stores she had on board?
A. Yes, but not the quantity without the manifest.
Q. Do you know what specie she carried?
A. Yes, there were 120 boxes of specie but I cannot say except from the manifest what each or all the boxes contained.
Q. What did they contain?
A. Some 10 000, some 5 000 and some less in pounds, some gold and some silver.
Q. Did the boats stay by the wreck till daylight?
A. No, but nearly till dawn.
Q. Was any attempt made to save anything?
A. No, the vessel floundered too quickly.
Q. Did you see Mr Brodie at any time?
A. No, but I heard his voice.
Q. Do you know the names of the look-out men?
A. Yes, Thomas Doyle on one bow and John Butcher on the other.
Q. How far do you estimate you were off the land?
A. About three miles, perhaps not so much.
Q. Do you know the bearing by compass of Danger Point?
A. No, I remember the true bearing was WxS.
Q. You said in your previous report you did not land in your own boat.
A. No, we were picked up by a sailing cutter.

Q. When the ship struck, what happened first – explain in detail.

A. When the ship struck I went on deck, and was just in time to hear the Commander tell all who could swim to jump. Just then the paddle box broke away, and some of the passengers on it.

Q. Were you on the ship when the fore part broke away?

A. Yes, but I left shortly after.

Q. Were you one of those who went to the wreck on the 29th?

A. Yes.

Q. Was the mast standing?

A. The topmast was gone, and the stump of the mainmast was just above water with the topsail yard.

Q. Why did you not try to recover the cargo and specie?

A. Because she was in too deep water.

Q. How deep was she?

A. In twelve fathoms.

Q. Could a diver not descend to twelve fathoms?

A. No, not over ten fathoms and then only in good water.

Q. Did you only go to her the once?

A. Yes, but the Surveyor and others went oftener.

Q. Did you see any bodies after they had been washed up?

A. Yes, a good many.

Q. What peculiarity did you notice?

A. I noticed that those who were nude were greatly eaten by sharks, while those that were dressed were mostly untouched.

Q. Is the tide and sea always rough?

A. No, one day it was so fine you could have gone to the wreck in a cask.

Q. Do you think any extra precautions could have been taken by the Commander?

A. No, I think everything that was possible both before and after the ship struck was done.

This was an amazing piece of information and has been copied in full as so much relating to the wreck is involved. The commander referred to was Captain Salmond. We now knew that 120 boxes of specie were on board when the *Birkenhead* sank.

More sleuthing revealed a letter written by Bernard Kilkeary who had been the paymaster-sergeant of the 73rd Regiment. Written 50 years after the event, the letter and reaction to it read as follows:

Above water-line plating

A number of shaving brushes

One of the compound portholes of the Birkenhead. The wooden section is missing

A brass porthole

A selection of hairbrushes and two toothbrushes

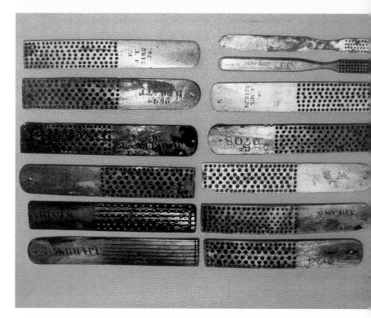

Webbing belt with two coins on the right

The Square, Dungannon
    Coy. Tyrone
        8th April 1902

Sir,

    Re Wreck of the Birkinhead

I beg respectfully to enclose for the perusal of the Rt. Honble the Secretary of State for War a Newspaper containing Narrative Supplied by me in Connexion with this Wreck, from which I have purposely omitted any reference to the "Specie" on Board which I understand was very considerable.

The information which I possess upon this subject I shall place at the disposal of the proper Government Department upon request being made to me.

I am Sir
    Your obedient servant
        (Sd) Bernard Kilkeary
        formerly Paymr. Sergt. 73 Regt.
        late Mid Ulster Artillery

The Under Secretary of State for War
    War Office Pall Mall
                London. S.W.

A Mr Marzial of the War Office forwarded this letter to the Treasury which responded:

W. to Fin. Sec. W.O.
26 April 1902

My Lord

I have laid before the Lords Commissioners of His Majesty's Treasury Mr Marzial's letter of the 19th instant (114/Misc:1336.(F1) forwarding a letter and enclosure (now returned herewith) from Mr B. Kilkeary respecting specie alleged to have been on board the troop-ship "Birkenhead" at the time when that vessel was wrecked in February 1852.

I am directed to refer to the correspondence noted in the margin, and to acquaint you for the information of the Secretary of State for War that, as a result of enquiries made in 1893, it was found to be impossible to say what amount of public treasure, if any, was on board the "Birkenhead" at the time of the wreck.

I am,
  My Lord
    Your obedient servant,
      Francis (unreadable)

The Financial Secretary,
  War Office.

In the original hand-written copy of 23 April 1902 a final paragraph states: 'My Lords do not consider that there would be any advantage in entering into communication with Mr (no name, presumably Kilkeary).'

I did attempt to find out what information Mr Kilkeary had. I wrote to the Black Watch (formerly the 73rd) in the hope of tracing a relative of Kilkeary who might have the papers, but the regiment unfortunately had no knowledge of the whereabouts of any living family. The matter has been left there.

The question of the missing stern was also an enigma that had to be resolved. It was possible to confine our salvage to the bows and engine-room, but as the bows were used as sleeping quarters and mess for the troops, not too much aside from cutlery, crockery and perhaps individual artefacts could be expected. All previous salvages would have concentrated on the bows and we could anticipate a virtually stripped zone. However, the magazine and a storage hold were also sited in the bows and hopefully these could be located, mapped and explored.

The Cape seas are not gentle. The currents can be very powerful and from time to time enormous storms whip the water into a frenzy. If there is a rock, the surging and pounding will soon make scrap of any ship unlucky enough to have been caught there. We had to face the probability that the portions of the Birkenhead that were known and had been worked on would be damaged beyond recognition, and the stern, if still in the area, could also be destroyed to the same extent. She could be broken into pieces and buried under tons and tons of sand and rocks rolled there during storms. We might not be able to recognise or identify any areas without some help.

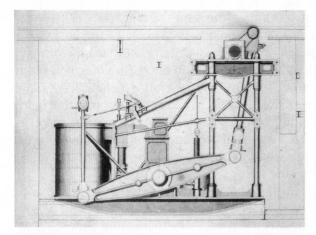

Plan of one of the two engines of the Birkenhead, *showing the single large piston, connected from its top to the large main beam which in turn drives the crankshaft to the paddle shaft (top right)*

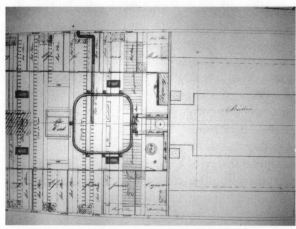

Middle deck plan showing boiler room as well as a carpenter's, gunner's and officers' cabins on the starboard side and boatswain's and officers' cabins to port

Plans were necessary. Once more I wrote to the National Army Museum. My request was forwarded to the National Maritime Museum and within a few weeks I had exact copies of the original plans of the *Birkenhead*. We could now see exactly where Alexander Seton had slept, where his toilet had been, where the officers had been quartered, and even where the troops had hung their caps. For hours we studied the plans, orientating and familiarising ourselves with the layout of the ship. We noted where the hatches had been, where the engine spares had been kept, where the ladders between decks had been, and where the women and children had eaten. Mentally I walked through the *Birkenhead*, visiting the ship's engineer in his cabin and the ship's doctor in his surgery. I entered the bread room and the lights room at the forward magazine. We believed that we would now be able to recognise fragments of the wreck.

It was essential that we locate the long missing stern section. It seemed obvious to us that a magnetometric survey of the area was a prime necessity. As none of us knew the first thing about magnetometry, the study of the variations and fluctuations in the earth's magnetic field, training was now required. The presence of a large metallic (especially iron) object in a magnetic field is likely to cause distortion of that field. So-called dipoles are induced which cause very characteristic patterns on a magnetic field chart. As the stern of an iron ship is a large object, we felt that scanning the area with a magnetometer would enable us, or at least help us, to find the stern.

I approached Anglo American's geophysical department and with great interest and enthusiasm for a novel project they supplied us with texts on the subject. So powerful is necessity that within a few days we were discussing field strengths with facility, and nanoteslas and secular variations became our friends. Meanwhile I got word that Aqua Exploration, a group of wreck divers in Cape Town, had a magnetometer. I was unable to negotiate the use of the instrument with them, but a seed had been planted in the person of one of their group, Charlie Shapiro.

It turned out that Charlie and his co-divers had been studying, examining and researching the *Birkenhead* for years. While diving and inspecting a historical wreck is perfectly legal, removing artefacts or undertaking any salvage without a permit is not. They had been unable to obtain the permit to salvage the wreck. I can imagine their chagrin and disappointment when they heard that a group of total unknowns from the Transvaal had obtained the rights to this most revered wreck.

The next thing we heard was that Aqua Exploration had found and identified the missing stern of the *Birkenhead!*

A message arrived that Aqua Exploration wanted to discuss the project with us. The very next day Charlie and Mike Keulemans of Aqua Exploration flew in from Cape Town and two days later a contract was signed between Depth Recovery Unit and Aqua Exploration. We had the diving equipment, the permit and masses of research, and they had the experience of years of wreck diving and detailed knowledge of the *Birkenhead* wreck, including the stern.

It is hard to describe the excitement, the satisfaction and the anticipation that I felt. The permit had been obtained, strong indication of the gold being on board had been found, and now the stern had been located. Very few people are fortunate enough to experience the thrill of being involved in great adventure.

Birkenhead Visited

In April 1984 our group travelled to the coast to meet the Cape half of our project and to see the wreck of the *Birkenhead*.

Under normal circumstances, the long drive to the Cape is a tiring and boring experience. Cruising along in my bright yellow Range Rover, the trip was a joy, however. I was finally going to see the *Birkenhead!*

We camped at a place with the unlikely name of Uilenkraalsmond, a little past the turn-off to Danger Point on the road to Cape Agulhas. A large, friendly and popular camping site, it is situated just off the beach. Together with Italo, Ken, Alan and Pierre I had spent years working on the diving chambers and read into the small hours of the mornings, scrutinising all the research. To be finally out in the open and about to dive into the sea again was magnificent.

The following morning found us ready and waiting for Charlie and the Aqua Exploration team. With Charlie were Mike Keulemans, Erik Lombard, André Hartman and Jimmy Herbert. With his close-cropped and curly light brown hair, Charlie is the backbone of the Aqua Exploration. Lean and slightly wolf-like in appearance, he has a quiet and withdrawn manner and, rare today, is a good listener. I was to become deeply impressed by his quest for perfection in drawings and sketches, his proficiency in photography and his methodical skill under water.

A little later we all left Kleinbaai, a small cove near Danger Point, in Charlie's boat *Sneaker*, bound for Birkenhead Rock.

A chain of rocks and reefs under shallow water projects out to sea from Danger Point. Towards the south-east the water depth increases to 28 m, and about 2 km from the point a single rocky pinnacle towers up towards the surface. Broad at its base, where it forms the southern wall of a sand-filled gully, the rock rises sharply, then shelves in before extending its 4-m broad, domed peak to within metres of the surface. When the sea is running high, both the reef and the lone peak are easily seen as the vicious breaks spray and foam over the rocks. It is a flat sea that hides the fang off Danger Point. With a calm sea no breaks

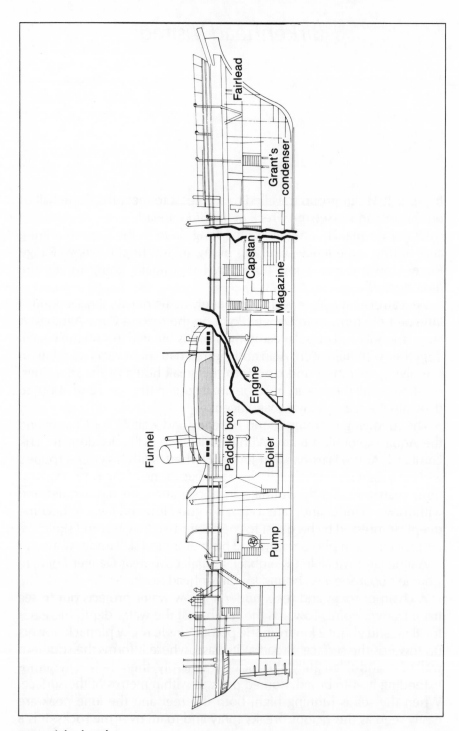

Sites of the breaks

occur and Birkenhead Rock is hidden under 3 m of placid water. Nothing marks the site of the pinnacle. These flat conditions were present when the *Birkenhead* struck the uncharted rock at 02h00 on the morning of 26 February 1852. Had the sea been rougher, the watch would undoubtedly have seen the massive curling break and heard its roar. Had the *Birkenhead* steamed a mere 6 m to either side, she would have missed the peak.

Togged up, air cylinders full, and trembling with anticipation, I watched Charlie guide the boat out to sea. Lazily the swells moved landwards from the south. The long smooth rollers so typical of the Cape seas lifted us high in the air for a moment, before dropping us into a blue-green trough. Further out, a small ruffle of white water sparkled, disappeared, then flashed again, becoming larger and larger as the land receded behind us. It was a lone wave. From a bulge of water it grew and broadened, developed an agitated crest of foam, then crashed over in a boiling arch. Sucking back, the water merged with the next approaching swell, fusing into its smoothness before adding to the bulge that appeared once more. Occasionally the wave grew to a towering mass and, drinking greedily from the water in its path, formed a deep pit into which it crashed, sending a white flurry of

Birkenhead Rock thrusting into the air

water over the surface. For an instant, at the moment before the break, a rounded brown lump thrust itself into the air between pit and wave. Like an enormous umber whale the rock surfaced, covered in red bait, mussels and barnacles, a domed peak that aired itself and quickly disappeared.

Awed, I gazed at the wave while the others busied themselves with weight belts, demand valves and fins. We were soon fully geared up and, rolling backward over the side of the boat, entered the cold green waters over the wreck of the *Birkenhead*. Down and down we swam, now part of the sea, free of the clumsiness of the weight of our equipment above the water, and oblivious of the wave that crashed above. Visibility near the surface is invariably bad in the area. Masses of plankton limit one's sight to only a few metres so that one becomes the centre of a turbid green silent sphere dropping down in the sea. One experiences a peculiar feeling of isolation, a sense of enclosure within a silent orb, only the reassuring whoosh of one's breathing breaking the illusion of total aloneness.

As we passed the 20-m mark the visibility suddenly opened up. There she lay, beam upon beam of encrusted metal, open ribs covered in sand, and tortuous, twisted and cavernous metal spaces everywhere. I was overwhelmed and stunned. Lying for a few moments on one of the shattered frames, I felt the *Birkenhead*, touched her and became fully aware of her destruction. For a while I was back with her moment of anguish, back at the instant of death and terror.

It was André who broke my reverie. Ebullient as ever, his lips wrapped around his demand valve in a grin, he touched my shoulder and signalled that we should follow him. We began a guided tour of the wreck, an overview of an era of over 130 years ago. Lying mostly buried under sand, the stern had been there all along. Broken, collapsed and covered, it had been the object of numerous salvage attempts,

Cleat at the bows

Paddle crankshaft

some official but most simply casual pilfering. Unrecognised and pre-
sumed lost, the stern lay precisely where it should have, behind the
gaping remnants of the boilers. So complete had the destruction been
that even the boilers were at first unrecognisable as such. They were
only a pile of twisted and shattered metal towering metres high above
the sandy floor. I had expected enormous damage but not total demolition.

Charlie had first found the bent and deformed tiller arm at the
extreme end of the wreckage and, poring over their plans, André had
recognised it for what it was. With this as reference point, the shape of
the broken curve of the stern plating, deeply covered in sand and
encrustation, snapped into focus. From the stern, we swam forward
over two of the cannons, passing the boilers and pausing at the large
empty sandy space that should have held the engines. On each side lay
a paddle wheel, now consisting only of a large, circular flywheel hub
attached to a massive drive shaft.

Curiously, I peered at the man-high hubs. The paddle blades were
missing. Clad in copper to resist corrosion, the blades had powered the
vessel when under steam. Looking more closely, I noticed thin strands

Tiller arm at the end of the stern

Paddle wheel hub and shaft

of plastic twisted and knotted near the shaft. Plastic? Not just plastic, but plastic-coated wire! The *Birkenhead* had been blasted for her copper, her brass and her contents. The copper cladding of her paddles had long since been smelted by an unknown looter. The reason for the demolition, rather than natural destruction, became obvious. Moving on, we reached the shattered bows, strewn over and up the base of the towering Birkenhead Rock.

Swimming back towards the stern, 70 m from the rock, we briefly explored the wreck. The *Birkenhead* is covered in coralline growth, her starkness muted by a century of calcific life. Fern coral, sponges and fish life thrive on this great ruin, creating beauty after calamity had passed.

At a depth of 28 m, our permitted 25 minutes of diving time passed in a flash. Because of the possibility of sharks we were loath to embark upon any decompression stops in those waters. One is most vulnerable at or near the surface where one is clearly outlined or silhouetted against the bright surface from below. A longer dive would entail stopping at a depth of 3 m or 6 m or both for a calculated time, while the excess nitrogen absorbed at depth is allowed to escape from the body via the exhaled air. The area near the *Birkenhead* is the home of the dreaded great white shark. Not far away is Dyer Island, the breeding place of thousands of seals and the seal pups are a rich source of food for the giant predators. We had no desire to pose as seals in our black wet suits while waiting for nitrogen to follow its concentration gradient!

We spent ten days at Uilenkraalsmond, diving on the *Birkenhead* and getting to know one another over barbeques and interminable discussions of our dives and the project. Our work on the wreck during this time was purely exploratory. It was necessary that we clearly define what our approach in practical terms was going to be. Sand and more sand was the main difficulty. This would have to be removed. Huge rocks tumbled on to the site by the sea were another problem.

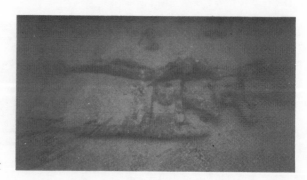

Sand covering the wreck

In order to divide the site into smaller working areas, some sort of grid pattern was necessary. In calm tropical waters a formal grid could be laid down of nylon ropes or aluminium tubes joined together in a series of squares. The water at the *Birkenhead* is not such a sea. Any attempt at a grid would be an exercise in futility. The currents would destroy the pattern within a few days at most. Guide ropes, knotted at intervals, were tied between the tiller arm and the paddle wheel area and from there to the bows. It is very easy to get hopelessly lost at the *Birkenhead*. Visibility is usually very limited. On occasion it can be as much as 20 m, but mostly it does not permit moving more than a few metres from the guide ropes without losing sight of them. Should one then swim around a little, more often than not one would be unable to find the wreck again, let alone the guide ropes. A slow ascent to the surface would reveal that one had drifted far from the wreck site. One could then either swim down the floating shot line again or return to the boat, depending on how much time had been spent under water.

Each diving day was followed by a period of active and often heated discussion. Charlie had by unspoken agreement become the cartographer of the project. When we first met him in Johannesburg, he had shown us his drawing of the area which had been compiled by observation of the wreck over many dives. Each of us would describe what he had seen and its relationship to the guide rope and Charlie would listen and mark a new stanchion, a piece of plating or even a rock on to his slowly developing drawing. The big difficulty was memory. At a depth of 30 m, a diver can still perform efficiently but the amount of nitrogen absorbed into his body and brain can take the edge off his intellectual capacity. This meant that details noted at depth were forgotten or blurred on returning to the surface. It was fascinating to hear how two divers in the same area could see quite different orientations of identical objects. 'The stanchion is just to the right of the bent plate,' said Alan. 'No, it's to the left,' said André, 'and the bent plate is further forward.'

This fogging of memory is called nitrogen narcosis, and is very similar to the effects of nitrous oxide used as an analgesic by dentists, or a few good tots of alcohol. It disappears during the ascent after the dive but makes observation and recall irritatingly laborious.

Erik or André would always dive first at the site to fix the marker buoy and assess the visibility and currents. Totally at ease, they would enter the water and disappear while the rest of the group waited in the boat for their decision. Sometimes the sea was very choppy and, sitting in the skiboat *Sneaker*, tossing and bouncing in the metres-high swell, I would cross my fins hoping for a 'no good' from them.

51

On one occasion the sea was absolutely flat, without even the smallest rise to mar its grey tranquillity, the sky obscured by a heavy fog. As we left Kleinbaai and sped along the water without the usual thump and bump of bouncing over swells, we were surrounded by a pale grey mist. We were the centre of a perfectly round clear area shrouded by a pallid orb of clouds. As we moved the circle moved with us, a magical canopy keeping our boat in the middle of an open hemisphere. Low in the east, the sun was a flat pale yellow disc flying through the fog with us. We could not find Birkenhead Rock. There was no wave, no noise, just a grey world above and pellucid water below which lapped and slushed against our glass fibre hull. We stopped to look and listen. From far away, through the fog at regular intervals came the lonely blast of the lighthouse. It was a moment of rare serenity for me, a time of isolation and strange peace. Ironically, it was those very sea conditions, without the fog, that caused the *Birkenhead* to strike and sink. Sitting in the boat I compared our tranquil state to the events of that night.

Getting Ready to Work

Back in Johannesburg, we had to decide how we would perform the salvage. We had seen and explored the wreck from stern to bows using scuba. The time available on a scuba dive was inadequate for the task ahead of us. Tons of sand would have to be moved, plate upon plate shifted and rocks displaced from their obstructing positions. An increased bottom time on the *Birkenhead* would mean performing decompression stops. No one was keen to do these stops in the water so they would have to be done immediately after leaving the water. The diver would be put into a recompression chamber on the deck of the ship and the chamber pressurised with air to the necessary depth for decompression. A gradual release of the pressure would then permit the diver to return to surface pressure. This method would mean that for a few minutes after leaving the sea and before entering the chamber for repressurisation our divers would be in danger of the bends.

A better method would be to use the diving bell we had built. On completion of their work on the wreck, divers could enter the bell at depth, close the hatches and be lifted to the surface still under pressure. They could then lock on to the prepressurised chamber on the ship and transfer to the chamber for decompression. There would be no period of low pressure and less risk of bending. The question was, could we use a diving bell so close to the rock, with the waves, turbulence and currents?

The divers would receive their air supply via a hose from the surface or from the diving bell. In this way their activities would not be limited by the amount of air available in a scuba cylinder. A low-pressure compressor on the ship would continuously fill a large storage tank to which the hoses to the divers would attach.

All this was simple. We could assemble and construct all the necessary piping, valving and so on. The biggest problem that now loomed was a suitable ship to carry our equipment. When complete it would weigh over 20 tons, which meant that a large vessel was needed. It would also have to carry at least twelve men and have facilities to feed them. All our money was disappearing into the building of the chambers. How were we to pay for the hire of a ship for months, an expense that could amount to thousands of rands per day? That was an easy one to answer – we couldn't. We had to convince a shipping company to join us in the venture on a no-cure-no-pay basis, which meant that if we found valuable and saleable items on the *Birkenhead* they would get a share. If we were unsuccessful, they would get nothing.

Sitting by the pool one day I thought about all this. Here we were, a group of men from Johannesburg, building our first diving system which we hoped would work but had not tested, planning to salvage a vessel that might or might not contain gold, and seeking a ship at no cost to ourselves, which had to moor next to a rock with a large wave constantly breaking over it. I began to get nervous. I had to hope that the people in shipping companies were as crazy as we were!

It was Ken de Goede who got the first interest from a shipping company. Ken is a stockbroker and working in the deafening din of the Johannesburg Stock Exchange he had built up a large number of contacts in a variety of different places. After speaking to a local shipping company with overseas representation, Ken casually told us that we could get a ship. Dirty, greasy and with spanner-bruised hands we clustered around him in the workshop while he lit one of his pulmonary challenges and blew a jet of black smoke into the air.

A fully equipped ship geared to salvage diving could be obtained and negotiations had been opened. The telex machine which I had installed at my home for rapid exchange of information began to chatter. Details of the wreck were required as well as a photographic survey. We then discovered that we had joined the ranks of the secretive. Divers are loath to discuss their work outside their group lest pirates should be given the opportunity to steal from their site. Un-willing to expose all the details obtained with so much effort until a formal agreement had been signed, we backed off. It was too easy to lose control of the expedition and the price in terms of a share was higher than we had anticipated.

A little wiser, I tried again. I hoped that Safmarine, one of the major shipping concerns in South Africa, would be interested in our aspira-tions. A letter explaining the broad outline of the project was sent and I waited. Nothing happened. I was later to learn that Safmarine is regu-larly badgered by cranks and parasites hoping for a free ship. Some muscle was needed. I put the problem to a friend who is highly respected in banking circles. He made a telephone call and lo, a door opened. I could make an appointment to explain what we were doing.

In mid-November 1984 Alan Holton, our legal authority, and I flew to Cape Town to convince a conservative and reputable company that they should anchor a multimillion-dollar ship next to a rock.

We were ushered into the office of Captain A.W. Blewett, the man in overall charge of shipping. Leaving us for a moment, he went to notify Captain Ockert Grapow who headed the tug division that we had arrived. Captain Grapow looked us over with a somewhat disconcerting gaze and waited for us to amuse him. Taking a deep breath I launched into the tale that I had practised so many times. Within a short time I saw that I had their interest and attention. Question after question was fired at us. Details of our work, permit, salvage licence and ability were tested and answered. I began to enjoy myself. More relaxed now and sensing a kindred spirit in Captain Grapow, I decided to go for broke and asked whether we could have a ship, please. The two captains looked at me and then at each other. Using a silent and secret method of communication known only to sailors and cormorants a decision was reached. 'Yes,' said Captain Grapow, 'let's go and see the *Wolraad Woltemade*. We'll meet at 14h00 hours at the berth.'

The *Wolraad Woltemade!* Named after a young man who had sacrificed his life rescuing people from another shipwreck by making trip after trip from the shore to the doomed vessel on his horse, the *Wolraad Woltemade* and its sister ship the *John Ross* are the two biggest tugs in the world!

Alan and I left the office in a daze. Waiting for the lift we were too scared to say anything in case someone changed his mind.

Outside the building, Italo, Charlie, Mike, Erik and André were waiting for us. 'Any luck?' asked Charlie. 'Sure,' I replied nonchalantly, 'we'll use the *Wolraad Woltemade*. It should be OK.' Dubiously they looked at us, waiting for the joke. Alan and I could contain ourselves no longer. Laughing and excited we related our meeting. Thereafter we all hastened to the docks, parked the car and approached the *Wolraad Woltemade*.

It was huge! Nearly a hundred metres long, its sleek black bows soared above the water and its snow-white superstructure underscored the power it possessed. We walked up and down the pier looking at the tug with unbelieving eyes. A sailor on board, seeing us leering at the vessel, the pride of Safmarine, asked, 'Can I help you?' 'No thanks,' we replied, 'we shall be using the *Wolraad* (now abbreviated because we owned her) for our salvage of the *Birkenhead*.' 'Oh!' he said and, shaking his head, turned and left us grinning on the shore.

At 14h00 sharp we met Captain Grapow and were treated to a tour of the vessel. It is an immaculate ship. I gazed at her enormous 14 400-kW engines with awe and at the great winches glistening with freshly greased steel ropes. In the control room state-of-the-art equipment greeted me in an almost surgically clean environment. I simply could not believe it. This was way in excess of my wildest expectations!

I cannot remember the flight back to Johannesburg, but the news we brought back was balm to Ken and Pierre. The last major hurdle, a ship, had been overcome. Contracts of agreement still had to be entered into but for the moment we were content. A few days before Christmas 1984 accord was reached. Safmarine would supply the surface craft, either the *John Ross* or the *Wolraad Woltemade*, depending upon which was available, and we would supply the divers, diving equipment and salvage technology.

The pressure to complete the diving system was now really on. All was arranged and it was up to us to get our equipment ready. As with so many projects, money was the problem. In order to speed up the work we needed to buy all the material at once. We approached a number of major companies for sponsorship or publicity rights, but none wanted to be involved with a salvage. Fear of a failed attempt, lack of public interest, or adverse publicity in terms of diver injury or death cautioned all of them away from us. We needed someone who would thrive on human drama. Ken approached the Argus Group who immediately responded to the idea. In early January 1985 the newspaper rights to the story of the salvage were given to the Argus Group. This was to prove a double-edged sword in that we received some desperately needed cash but the ensuing publicity was to cause us great distress.

Brass telescope, badge of the 43rd Regiment, R. Sheldon-Bond's nameplate, gold and silver coins

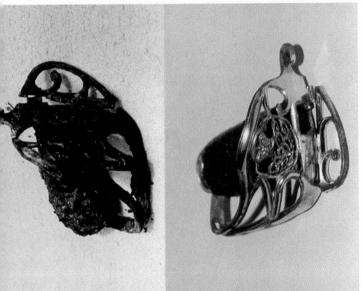

Sword hilt before and after restoration

Pewter syringes found in ship's surgery

Doorknobs

Portion of sword hilt in conglomerate

A Time of Strife

On 6 January 1985 the front page of *The Sunday Star* in Johannesburg carried a report headlined 'Divers poised to raise sunken hoard', the *Weekend Argus* in Cape Town one headlined 'Cape hunt for gold fortune', while the *Sunday Tribune* in Durban reported on a 'R40m gold hunt'. All three papers had a picture of our group with a porthole off the *Birkenhead*. Every week for the next three and a half months our project received wide press coverage.

Argus *photograph of Depth Recovery Unit team and porthole*

At that stage we were not nearly ready even to begin the work but the Argus newspapers were worried that the news of our impending salvage would leak and they would lose the impact of the story.

At that point I had spent two years researching the wreck, contacting the regiments and convincing the authorities that we could perform a reputable salvage. All this was to be threatened by the publicity, but we were powerless. We had to finance the work and had to accept whatever was to come. Come it did and in a two-pronged attack. A direct onslaught from the archaeological establishment hit the news within weeks, followed by a more indirect challenge from the British with regard to ownership.

Ironically, not one of our critics came to see us, our chambers or bell, or the thousands of words of painstaking research that we had prepared. We were accused of mining the wreck, looting and having 'to work fast because of the expense and could not record all that archaeologists would want to know in a month or more'. An honorary curator of the National Monuments Council resigned because, among other reasons, we were going to plunder the wreck.

Archaeological experts reacted strongly. They seemed convinced that we were going to concentrate only on that part which may contain the coinage. A letter in the press stated, 'This (a proper salvage) would be at least several years work (is it part of the contract to complete the work?)' For some reason it was assumed that we would strike the wreck, rip out what we could and leave. The letter continued: 'Real archaeologists, not necessarily today, but in the near future, might want to have *detailed* information on the structure of the craft, layout of facilities for each stratum of the hierarchy aboard this military vessel, i.e. sailors, soldiers, officers, women and children, and the associated artefacts to give an idea of the conditions which may have resulted in the loss of so much life. The detailed relationships of the pieces to each other may offer other social data to understand how the people related to each other. There are potentially many questions that could be answered by careful strategy, all of which would require time. An adequate excavation cannot be accomplished in one month or two. The papers have mentioned that a contract may be signed with SAF-MARINE for the use of a tug as a diving platform, a vessel that costs R250 000 per month to hire. At this cost they must remove the overlying materials as fast as possible until they can be sure the coinage is aboard. No one will really accept that the cultural priorities take precedence when there is a reputed king's ransom of possibly greater than 30 million Rand in gold to be mined.'

I was devastated when asked by the media to comment on this. For over a year I had pored over the original plans of the *Birkenhead*, noting and correlating the layout of facilities available for the people aboard. To conclude from a press report that we would spend one or two months on the work was unjustified and unworthy. The hire of a tug from Safmarine and the fact that we would have to hurry to justify R250 000 a month (where did that figure come from?) was sheer fantasy.

We were still in Johannesburg perfecting our equipment and were to continue to do so for another year before even commencing the salvage. Week after week we read the mounting criticism of our activities and plans with growing distress. We had not even begun and had been severely prejudged.

Still, no one who became embroiled in the weekly saga in the press approached us directly. We decided to maintain total discretion and refrained from becoming involved in the debacle.

Over one year before, in early 1984, I had approached the Professor of Archaeology at the University of Cape Town for advice on conservation and restoration and, following his response and good wishes with the project, had begun earnest research into these aspects.

Obviously, we would have liked to find gold. I do not believe that any salvor or archaeologist would readily pass up the possibility of finding a fortune in gold coinage. But we had pledged to perform a full survey and recovery of the wreck, including cultural, historical, and archaeological aspects. We had not set a time limit or a limit on the extent of our work. In our negotiations with Safmarine the fact that a scientifically acceptable salvage was mandatory was clearly understood. We were prepared to offer our all, as was Safmarine. This simple fact, that the *Birkenhead* would be examined as closely as possible, was just not believed.

The Department of Manpower then contacted me. A chief inspector in Pretoria telephoned me one day to inform me that we were about to contravene the provisions of the Machinery and Occupational Safety Act as amended in 1984. The Act provides that the moment any remuneration is obtained in diving, the project is considered underwater building work and only commercially qualified divers may perform the salvage. In addition, a qualified diving supervisor has to be present at all times. Our team of divers, although very experienced in wreck location, assessment and salvage failed to meet this requirement. None of us were commercial divers. Most commercial divers, on the other hand, have very little experience of the techniques of wreck diving.

I was shaken by this new dilemma. We simply could not change our team. Our various areas of expertise were essential for the work. Alan Holton obtained a copy of the Act and verified what I had been told. As we read through the requirements, the glimmering of an idea began to form. Apart from diver training requirements, the Act also spelled out the prerequisites for the establishment of a commercial diving school – adequate chamber facilities, compressors and the rest of the usual equipment. Standing next to our diving bell and decompression chamber complex, the solution was obvious. We already had the best diving equipment and facilities. Our technology was in excess of the requirements of a school. What we would need were a diving instructor and supervisor. A supervisor was mandatory anyway, so only an instructor would be needed as an extra team member. All our divers could then register as learner commercial divers and the salvage could continue under the guidance of an instructor and supervisor.

When we approached the Department of Manpower for permission to register as a commercial diving school, we were met with friendly courtesy. Our application proceeded without a hitch and Depth Recovery Unit Diving School was born. An unexpected branch had grown and was to develop into a full-time school in the lay-up basin of Cape Town harbour.

During this period communications and telexes were flying almost daily between Captain Grapow in Cape Town and me. Hundreds of issues had to be resolved. Three-phase power had to be available at 380 volts. Water was needed, as well as winch power and crane facilities for the bell, low-pressure air for the lift pumps, food for the divers, and accommodation on board. Italo Martinengo as usual took charge of the electromechanical requirements on our side. He began designing cranes and A-frames, big and versatile enough to handle a diving bell and its occupants in a choppy Cape swell.

During April the press reports tailed off and finally stopped as it became clear that we would not be taking our diving bell and chambers to the Cape in 1985. Heaving sighs of relief, we packed our dive bags and once more journeyed to the site of the *Birkenhead*. We were anxious to scuba dive again but, more important, the *John Ross* would be sailing from Cape Town to assess the site.

It was to be only a ten-day visit to determine exactly where we would put our chambers on the ship, how we would use the facilities, and how the vessel would moor at Birkenhead Rock. Leaving Johannesburg on the midnight flight, we were excited at the prospect of seeing the wreck after a year's absence.

Descending through the now familiar limbo of green water, we once more examined the wreck. Each time one visits the *Birkenhead* the scene changes. We found that sand had covered plates and wreckage previously exposed, and previously hidden areas were uncovered. Pierre and I were diving near the bows when we came across a large rectangular gleaming copper box half buried in the sand. Looking at

60

each other wide-eyed through our masks, we had a common thought. We had found a treasure chest! The top of the box was damaged and, peering through the cracks, we saw tube after tube in neat alignment with sand filling all the gaps. No treasure chest, but Grant's condenser used on the *Birkenhead* to supply fresh water by condensing boiler steam!

Each day brought new orientation and this was what we most needed before even beginning any work. A broken blue and white plate, immovably imbedded in conglomerate became a marker, a pink coral fern another. Thus, a series of landmarks was established which made for increasingly accurate orientation on the shattered maze-like ruin. Nothing was recognisable. There were no decks, no intact hull, no entrance into anything. The wreck was flat, collapsed and buried. Between corroded and conglomerated beams the feelers of dozens of crayfish tested the water, hurriedly withdrawing on our approach. Red romans swam idly through the open spaces between frames and hottentots (a species of fish) moved warily around us.

Grant's condenser
appearing as a
'treasure chest'

On one occasion I was with Italo. Sifting by hand through the sand he found two intact and corked wine bottles. Holding the dark brown bottles up, we saw that they still contained wine. This was excitement indeed and, comparing our position with the plans, we saw that we had been at the remains of the spirit room. It was only weeks later that the implication hit me. The spirit room was in the lower decks of the vessel. If we had been there, where were the upper two decks? Why had we found no trace of them?

Towards the beginning of May the *John Ross* appeared over the horizon and, with twin arches of water surging at the bows and a great boil of sea astern, the tug approached Birkenhead Rock. Her captain, a wise and careful man, dropped anchor while still far from the rock after a constant sounding for depth on his approach. His objective was to see how close the *John Ross* could approach the rock in safety. Using one of her powerful boats he surveyed the area, made his measurements and, rather quickly I thought, returned to the *John Ross*.

His comment to us a little later was very succinct. 'Not a chance, you guys are bloody nuts!' The ship was too big. An approach close enough for us to dive with our equipment would place the bows past the rock. Any lateral movement would then cause the hull to hit the peak. Once more I felt the so familiar clutch of rejection and disappointment. We did not have a ship any more. I had been so sure of the huge black-hulled vessels, so confident in their ability. They were the greatest tugs in the world. That a mere rock should daunt them was unthinkable. We had been to the area, even over the rock in a fog, in a thin glass fibre boat. The titans could not go where we had frolicked.

By this time Captain Grapow and I had built up a sort of telex-pal relationship. We had met only a few times, but the constant communications had changed from a very formal tone to an increasingly relaxed one. When news of the inspection reached him, he said (as he was to say again and again), 'No problem'. When Captain Grapow says 'No problem', there is none! He simply changed tack. Unbeknown to us, negotiations between Safmarine and Land & Marine were already afoot to form Pentow Marine. The tug *Causeway Adventurer*, smaller than the *John Ross* and *Wolraad Woltemade* but equipped with all the facilities, was made available to us.

Yet another hurdle was waiting on my return to Johannesburg. The wide news coverage we had received had come to the attention of the British Admiralty. When my receptionist told me that the Department of Foreign Affairs was on the phone, I wanted to run away. There was no chance I was going to be invited to a formal do or receive a medal. It had to concern the *Birkenhead*. A very polite voice told me that it was indeed in connection with the *Birkenhead* that he was phoning. Could I please make an appointment to discuss British interest in the wreck at the Union Buildings in Pretoria? What new trouble awaited?

Rob Durno, my pal and father-in-law, accompanied me to Pretoria for moral support. Clutching my I.D. book in case it was needed, I entered the sanctum sanctorum and approached the security desk. 'I.D. book, please.' I was ushered into a room that looked like a government room and sat down.

The meeting was very pleasant and informal. I described our work and the wreck, and over a cup of weak tea was informed that we had the full backing of the South African authorities. Now that was really nice. I then realised that the authorities had in fact been most supportive all along. The National Monuments Council had given us our permit, the Department of Customs and Excise our salvage licence, the Department of Manpower advice and help in the formation of our school, and now the Department of Foreign Affairs was assisting us on the issue of British interest in the *Birkenhead*.

As the story was related to me I began to feel as if I was going to be responsible for the next Anglo-Boer War. About six months after we had received permission to salvage the *Birkenhead*, the British government had approached the Department of Foreign Affairs through their embassy.

The department was informed that it was United Kingdom practice to maintain all rights and interests in British warships and other non-commercial ships wherever they may lie until official notice of abandonment was announced by the British government.

After investigating our permit, the department had informed the British Embassy that the *Birkenhead* had ceased to be the property of the British government. One year later, following the enormous news coverage, the British government repeated their claim of ownership and the South African government reaffirmed their position. Both countries claimed ownership and there I was with a permit in my hand, our equipment incomplete, the salvage not yet commenced, and being called a looter and miner in the papers.

While driving back to Johannesburg, I was pleased that we had local official sanction to continue but wondered where all this would eventually lead. If the salvage yielded only artefacts and naval memorabilia there would not really be any difficulty, but if we found gold in any quantity the sparks would fly. I had confirmed time and again that there was no official record of any gold coinage aboard the vessel, but if we did locate sovereigns, I envisioned a protracted battle which could take years to resolve. It was essential that the question of ownership be resolved in advance, as it would be very difficult to obtain agreement after possibly millions in gold had been recovered.

After discussing the problem among ourselves, it was decided to obtain our own legal opinion from British and South African experts in the field. The opinion was unanimous. All our advisers regarded the wreck as the property of the British government.

The Department of Foreign Affairs was again approached. Following a second meeting, the wreck was again confirmed as being within the exclusive jurisdiction of the South African government. The British

Crown could neither authorise nor deny salvage rights on South African national monuments, nor forbid diving within South African waters. We could accept this, but would the British government? The answer was no.

They were concerned about the war grave aspect of the salvage. The *Birkenhead* had never been officially declared a war grave, but the issue was extremely sensitive as she had become an integral part of British maritime tradition and the watery grave of her soldiers was revered, with or without an official writ. They were worried that we would surface from the water one day with the bones of their soldiers and that the press would have a field day with the news. In order to allay this fear, I wrote to the British Ministry of Defence assuring them that this would never happen. We were conscious of the sensitivity of the issue and should any remains be found they would be treated with great respect and left strictly alone. After all, we had been exposed to so much antagonism that to feed the fires by promoting sensationalism was the last thing we would wish to do.

With the issue of ownership unresolved, working at our separate livelihoods every day and on the chambers every night and weekend, we slowly reached the point where our chambers, bell and masses of equipment were finally ready to travel. It had taken us over three years to reach that moment.

The *Birkenhead* was waiting for us. It had carved a place for itself in history as one of man's greatest moments of self-sacrifice and heroism. A struggle had been anticipated when our initial planning began, and we were now ready and honoured to begin the most significant salvage operation in South African history.

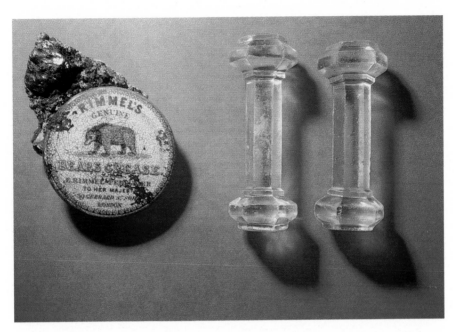

Porcelain lid ('Rimmel's genuine bear grease') and two crystal knife and fork supports for use at table

Decorative chin chain with lion's head, two badges and thistle

Bronze double pulley with broad arrows

Ornamental chain with lion's head partially cleared of conglomerate

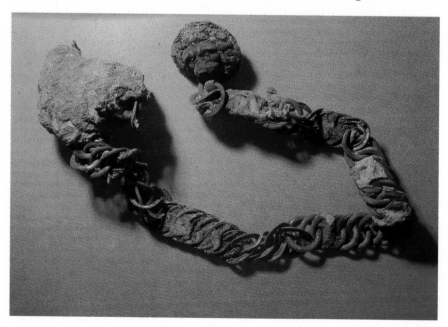

Tetrahedral skylight

Pipe fragments, stem and bowl

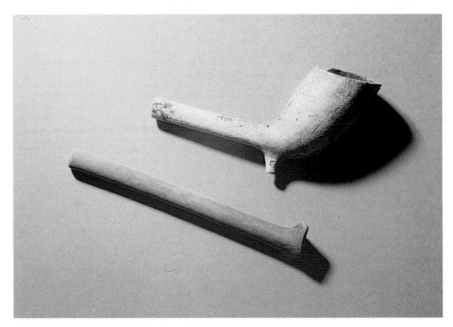

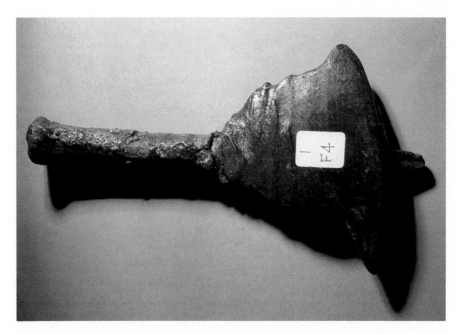

Copper nail in worn piece of decking – the first artefact raised

Rowlock from stern quarter-deck area (probably from the cutter with the women and children), and a pulley wheel showing two broad arrows

The Salvage Begins

On 6 January 1986 two huge articulated flat-bed vehicles left Alfirevich Transport bearing our diving complex *en route* for Cape Town harbour.

Moving on to truck en route to Cape Town

Steeling ourselves for the furore that would follow the news of our departure, we made the hot 1 500-km trip and waited at Table Bay for the trucks to arrive. Tired and grubby, Alan Holton and Pierre Joubert, who had accompanied the chambers, entered the customs area at the docks with triumphant grins. Our happiness that the system was eventually where it belonged was so infectious that even the customs people were enthusiastic. Slowly and sedately a procession of cars and trucks made its way to where the *Causeway Adventurer* was waiting, her large stern deck cleared and ready for us.

'SA divers all set for golden bonanza from treasure ship', 'Off to a seabed Eldorado' shouted the headlines. Putting the newspaper down, I joined the ant-like activity on the *Causeway Adventurer*. There was much to do. Sensational reporting could wait.

On the dock the indefatigable Italo was in charge. The huge A-frame for lifting and lowering the bell was being fitted to the system. The giant rams were extended and their heavy ends connected to the closely machined supports with glistening hard-chromed and ground shafts. A mammoth crane, which dwarfed even our fifteen tons of chambers, slowly lowered its huge hook. High-tensile chains shackled to our unit tautened and pinged as the crane took the strain. Gradually the yellow and black diving equipment rose into the air. With anxious hands correcting any tendency to swing, the crane arm moved across and then over the stern of the *Causeway Adventurer*. A moment to align, a shouted 'Down, down!' and it was done.

The men of Aqua Exploration and the crew of the ship were all there to help. Charlie and Italo took on the task of welding the entire support frame on to a dozen I-beams, which in turn had to be welded to the deck of the ship. This involved days of backbreaking work, bruising, cuts and burns. We had to be sure that the heavy chambers would not move, even in a high sea with the vessel rolling and pitching. If tons of steel were to begin sliding on deck it would be disastrous and we could wave goodbye to everything.

While Charlie and Italo were creating lumbar disc problems, the rest of us were manhandling into place the 96 extra-large cylinders of oxygen we would need for decompression. Two huge air banks, each weighing over a ton, were secured and chained into position. Gas and air hosing had to be completed. Every day Mike and I went shopping for couplings, valves, bolts and a myriad of accessories.

We were accompanied by Malcolm Ferguson who had joined the project as our commercial diving supervisor in accordance with the requirements of the Department of Manpower. Tall and in his mid-thirties, he had short dark hair. His experience in Brazilian waters and the North Sea at depths exceeding 300 m was vast and we were a little in awe of him. As this was his first real wreck salvage experience, he was both intrigued and excited by the riddles posed by the *Birkenhead*.

The chief engineer, a large blond Norwegian who said that he was a 'Wiking' and that his name was unpronounceable for us and simply called himself Stein ('like the wine') came over to our group. The late

Cape twilight had set in and we were labouring furiously to complete the installation on board. 'Is dere anyting else you need me for?' shouted Stein. Stein always shouted. 'No,' said Malcolm, 'Goodbye!' 'If you don't need me any more tell me to go to hell,' shouted Stein. 'Go to hell!' said Malcolm, clearly enunciating each word and coolly continuing his work. The entire deck became quiet. Even Stein forgot to shout. We all looked at each other, stunned and surprised, then collapsed with laughter. Malcolm blithely went on with what he was doing, totally unruffled and with characteristic poise. This became a routine. Every night Stein would climb from his immaculately kept engine-room, his T-shirt tightly stretched over his Viking belly and once-white shorts, approach Malcolm and, peering short-sightedly at him through gold-framed spectacles, bellow, 'Goot-night!' 'Go to hell!' Malcolm would reply.

A registered instructor now had to be appointed to the team so that the divers, now officially registered as learner commercial divers, could perform diving work. Konrad Stutterheim joined us. In his late thirties, Konrad has a cat-like agility and grace of movement. In a huge swell, he could leap from a ski-boat to the gunwales of the *Adventurer* quite effortlessly. I was to envy him this ability on many occasions as I clawed my way on to the ship from a ski-boat or inflatable, losing a shoe or tearing my shirt with my scrabbling, scuttling technique of embarkation.

He too had extensive diving experience and his ability under water was equal to his nimbleness above. He was to become fascinated by the *Birkenhead* and enormously intrigued by the dark black conglomerate that dominated the stern of the wreck.

We worked at the docks for twenty days from sunrise to dusk to complete all that had to be done. The hot-water machine that would draw up sea water at the wreck site, heat it and then pump it down to the divers' suits for warmth had to be purchased and modified. The umbilical hoses that would carry the divers' air supply and hot water had to be bought and twisted together in a giant plait. End couplings had to be fitted, compressors mounted and tested. Electricity had to be supplied to the control cabin, and power to all our motors. Day after day we toiled, lashed by a south-easter that carried masses of fine shot from the shot-blasters in the dry dock into our faces, eyes and ears. Several times a day the heavy coating of black dust had to be swept away and dumped.

When we first tested the bell by lowering it into the water at the pier it floated! Ruefully we looked at each other. We had anticipated that this might happen, but had been unable to weigh the bell. Despite its

67

thick walls and heavy steel ballast, it required two tons of lead to ensure that it would behave like a submersible and not like a bright yellow buoy.

On our second test the bell behaved magnificently. The *Causeway Adventurer* fired up her engines and we moved out of the harbour towards Robben Island. Dropping anchor, the *Adventurer*, under the watchful eye of Clive Gibson, her captain, waited for us to test the system at sea.

The heavy steel wire rope that was to lower and lift the bell was already looped over the large pulley on the A-frame and connected to the massive winch of the tug. High above in the control cabin the ruddy face of Stein peered down at us, his hands on the winch controls. Over the ship's loudspeaker his voice roared at us, 'Waa ta! blaa mawa!' It was impossible to understand him and we changed to hand signals.

The familiar whine of the hydraulic power pack started and Italo with great care shifted the levers to move the large arms of the frame outwards over the stern, the bell firmly clamped in the holding cradle. As the rams reached full extension, he released the locking jaws that fixed the bell. Sliding down its two guide wires, the bell descended into the sea. There was a moment of frothing as it penetrated the surface and then it was gone from sight. Over the communications the divers inside reported their gauge pressures while in the control cabin I compared the readings with the topside pneumofathometer read-out. Pressurising the inside of the bell to equal the outside water pressure proceeded smoothly and, at 20 m, the external hatch opened and two divers left the bell breathing from their umbilical connections.

After twenty minutes, the divers returned to the bell and closed the hatches. Gently Stein started the winches again, this time hauling the bell back to the surface and up to the waiting cradle which received and locked on to the bell as smoothly as silk. The return to deck and mating with the deck decompression chamber also proceeded flaw-lessly.

We had proved ourselves but there was no excited chatter or back-patting. A determination had taken over as soon as we saw that we could win. We were ready for our expedition; we had waited long enough. Laird's famous *Birkenhead*, once so maligned for her iron hull, awaited us with our steel-hulled ship, hard-chromed rams and tungsten-tipped tools.

In the meantime the *Causeway Salvor*, the *Adventurer*'s sister ship, had been busy. She was to drop the seven-ton anchors attached to heavy chain, steel rope and buoys that we would need to moor at the site of the wreck. On her stern the three anchors lay, their flukes encrusted with barnacles from previous work but more than ready to take the load we required.

On Wednesday 29 January both the *Causeway Adventurer* and the *Causeway Salvor* moved slowly out of the harbour bound for Danger Point and the *Birkenhead*. They left at night in order to reach their destination early the next morning.

Early in the morning the Aqua team, Italo, and I left Gansbaai by ski-boat and sped over the swells towards the wreck, racing over each crest and dropping heavy-stomached into each trough. The tugs had both arrived and were at anchor. The *Salvor*, as if impatient to begin her work, was just south of Birkenhead Rock, her bows into the current and rolling slowly from side to side. The *Adventurer* with our bright yellow chambers now washed clean of harbour dust, waited about 2 km to the west. A brisk south-easter was blowing and there was a choppy swell. We approached the *Adventurer* in Italo's twin-hulled ski-boat *Splash Dance*. Clive Gibson was waiting for us. Motoring into the lee of the vessel, we paused while he timed the swell and leapt nimbly aboard our ski-boat. He was to assess the site and we were to drop marker buoys for the *Salvor* to release the king-sized anchors. Mike had already ensured that the buoys were ready and weighted. We circled the area, passing close to the wave then further out, round and round, again and again, until Clive was satisfied. Then we dropped the three markers in rapid succession, one close to the rock and just south-east of the pinnacle, another south of the rock, and a third to the west.

We were really there. All those months and years of research, planning, correspondence, toil, failures, successes, dreams, hopes, and almost impossible negotiations were finally merging. Two large tugs waited for us to begin the final chapter of the *Birkenhead* saga. We had dreamed a dream of magnificent adventure and excitement on a splendid scale and here we were!

The day before Clive Gibson had told me that we had only two days to drop the anchor buoys for our moorings. If the weather was bad, we would have to wait a week as the *Salvor* was needed elsewhere. As if on order, the wind suddenly settled and the swell began to diminish visibly. That day the *Causeway Salvor* dropped the three seven-ton anchors and many tons of chain. The first and most difficult was the south-east anchor, only about 50 m from the rock.

While the tug backed in steadily from the south, her powerful bow thrusters guided and pushed her towards the bobbing red buoy we had dropped to mark the position. Captain Rick Wilson almost nonchalantly and with superlative ease manoeuvred the maroon-hulled tug to the marker buoy, with the massive break over Birkenhead Rock roaring on her starboard side. She was making the closest approach to the rock in 134 years. The first anchor rattled over the stern roller, followed by metres and metres of the heaviest gauge chain that Pentow Marine could muster. Thick steel wire followed the chain, and finally the hulking black buoy plunged over the stern to begin its dance next to the rocky peak. It veered nearer to the rock with each break in the opalescent foaming circle that formed after the passage of the wave, then skipped further away as a dark hump of water hunched and reared up before smashing itself in an eternal attack on the unyielding peak. We were spellbound. Watching us through binoculars the lighthouse keeper at Danger Point sounded his foghorn, a deep and blunted blast that reverberated again and again, to applaud our minor victory over the fang that had claimed all those lives.

The south buoy further from the rock followed rapidly, and finally the west buoy completed a trio of moorings bouncing and cavorting around Birkenhead Rock.

We were going to dive over the stern of the tug. Because of the length of the vessel we could not moor with the bows of the ship into the swell as the bows would then be perilously close to the rock. Our only choice was to moor stern-on to the elements. This meant that we were in for a bumpy slamming ride, but spirits were high and our hearts afire.

The laying of the moorings had taken two hours, not two days. As we gazed on the buoys, the weather worsened and the sea became angry, the rock emerging time after time from beneath its thundering wave, as if to see those who would dare challenge its domain.

Excited and exuberant, we clambered aboard the *Adventurer* and watched the *Salvor* as she turned to begin her trip back to Cape Town.

The *Causeway Adventurer*, although much smaller than the giant *Wolraad Woltemade* and *John Ross* tugs, was still too big to enter Gansbaai harbour, and anchoring permanently on site at the rock was too dangerous. If one of the mooring ropes parted, the tug would be on the rock within seconds. Clive decided that each day after finishing work we would haul in the ropes, lift anchor and move into Walker Bay where a much calmer and protected anchorage was available for the night. Every morning we would return to the site, drop the bow anchor and move backward towards the rock. The mooring ropes had to be towed by ski-boat to the buoys and shackled to them to give a three-point mooring, the bow anchor towards land while the position of the other two buoys would depend upon the current and the wind.

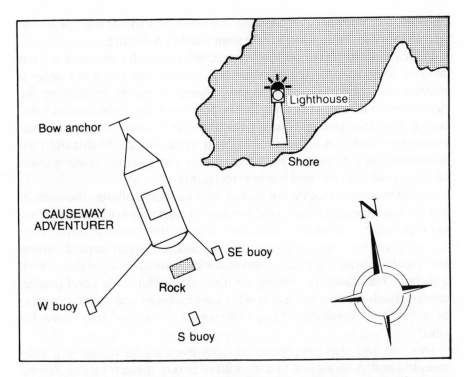

Accommodation on board was insufficient for all of us, so for the next few months Gansbaai was to be home for most of the team. It is a small sleepy place and within hours the entire community knew of us. We became known as 'die duikers'.

Right next to the fish factory is a concrete slipway and it was from there that we were to leave by ski-boat every morning at 05h00 bound for the *Adventurer* at anchor in the bay. Charlie had bought a new boat. The ski-boat *Sneaker* had been replaced by a catamaran called *Seaker*, a change in tone for the better, I thought. Huddled together in the pre-dawn darkness and shivering with cold, we would wait for Charlie and Mike to launch *Seaker* and come alongside the pier.

At the end of the early morning trip to the tug we had to leap from the boat to the deck of the tug 2 m above the ski-boat. The trick was to wait for the swell to lift the little boat up and jump at the peak just before the boat dropped again. Mostly it worked, but sometimes it did not and an élite club of early morning bathers grew in numbers.

Charlie, Mike and the bravest souls would speed off in *Seaker* to the wreck to await the arrival of the *Adventurer* and the dawn, before hauling the heavy blue mooring ropes to the buoys. The rest of us would race to the galley for a splendid breakfast, hot coffee and fresh toast, while the rattle of anchors being lifted and chain being stowed signalled our imminent departure. The noise of anchors was the wake-up call for Alan, Pierre and Ken in their bunks on the tug.

With a second cup of coffee in my hand, I made for the deck to start the compressors, pressurise the air storage tank and bring the decompression chamber to correct depth. Malcolm would be starting the hot-water machine, checking the temperature of the water and ensuring that everything was set for the day's work. A routine was established that was to become second nature to all. At first light we assembled on the stern to help with the mooring ropes, passing them to *Seaker* with its cold and hungry occupants.

As the mooring ropes were pulled tight by their bollards, the motion of the ship changed drastically. She was at best a heavy roller and her tall topmast would swing right over to port, then back again to starboard. Once held by the ropes, the *Adventurer* began to pitch, lifting her flat aft bottom high out of the water before slamming it down with a thump. Naturally the rolling continued as well. This combination caused much distress to visitors who later came to watch our progress on a weekend. Invariably they would spend the whole day praying for land!

This rise and slap prevented us from even trying to use our submersible bell. A sequence of a slow lift of two to three metres followed by a smack down made bell launching and retrieval from the turbulent water too tricky and dangerous. Our other two chambers, the entrance lock and the decompression chamber, both firmly welded to the deck of the *Adventurer*, were our only option unless we used special mixes of nitrogen and oxygen.

We would dive directly off the vessel, descend to the *Birkenhead* for the work period of 80 minutes and then ascend to the surface. At the surface the diver would be heavily overloaded with nitrogen gas, which would begin boiling out of solution in his blood and tissues within a few minutes. He had to get aboard the tug as quickly as possible where waiting hands were ready to strip his suit and gear from him with speed. Then into our chamber entrance lock where fast pressurisation ensured that the nitrogen remained dissolved followed by a transfer through the steel hatch into the main chamber, and finally the slow decompression. A delay of only a few minutes from surfacing to recompression would guarantee the bends. The method is far from ideal and potentially dangerous, but we were to get it down to a fine art.

Diving began on 31 January 1986. Scuba only was used on the first dive as we had once more to familiarise ourselves with the lie of the wreck. Moreover, neither Malcolm nor Konrad had ever seen the

72

Thermometer backing plate, graduated in °F and body heat

Solid silver earpick used to remove ear wax

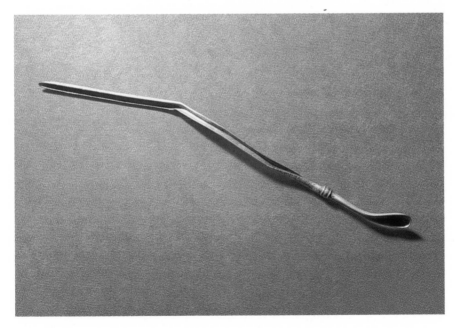

The supporting eye of the Birkenhead bell. No other remains were found

Cleaned copper powder flask with brass top and untreated copper birdshot holder

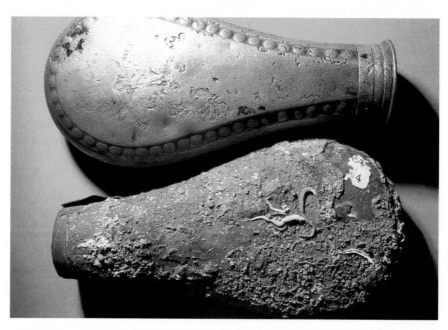

Birkenhead. Erik and André dived first to place the red marker buoys on the stern, boiler section and bows, and then to tie a guide rope between these on the wreck.

Within a few minutes three markers were dancing in the swell, tied by their polypropylene ropes to the various areas of the wreck. In pairs, the other divers leaped from the stern, pushing far out with a giant stride and making for the stern buoy. They would pause for a moment to check their orientation before they duck-dived down to the *Birkenhead*. Down and down, the yellow rope their guide as it appeared metre after metre into the green haze surrounding them. An instant of quick cold signalled a thermocline, a layer of icy cold water below relatively warmer water. Finally they reached the sandy bottom, turning to gaze at the destruction around them.

Both Malcolm and Konrad were amazed by the *Birkenhead*. Like us, their initial impression was one of chaos and confusion with no possibility of identifying anything. The *Birkenhead* does not yield her secrets readily. Repeated diving and observation were essential before any semblance of order became apparent. Charlie, who was most aware of this, was to make dive after dive taking measurement after measurement, slowly adding to his drawings with infinite patience and care.

The *Birkenhead* had come to rest in a gully at the foot of Birkenhead Rock. Following her breakup on the surface, the various pieces were distributed over a large area, 75 m by 54 m. During the previous season we had already determined that it was impossible to lay a standard physical grid over such an area next to the rock. We would have to utilise direct measurements of distance between selected objects, such as points on the tiller arm, cannons, boiler and paddles, to establish a series of triangles which could then be plotted on paper. The paper was divided into 450 squares, 25 across and 18 down, each 3 cm square. One centimetre represented one metre. The squares across were designated A to Y and down 1 to 18. We could then identify any part of the wreck in a 3-m square area, for example B11 or H4. It was decided that we would begin the work at the stern and investigate the section E to G, 4 to 5. More precise mapping was now needed. Charlie expanded the scale on a secondary grid, with two centimetres representing one metre and each square being divided into nine smaller squares numbered one to nine. An artefact found in F4 could now be pinned to F4-7, an area only 1 m by 1 m on the wreck and 2 cm square on the plan. By directly measuring on the bottom with a graduated plastic tape and recording the result with a pencil on a sanded perspex plate we could plot the exact point within the little square. We had a workable grid without fighting the sea.

Mike took charge of the notation of the artefacts. As each artefact was raised, it received a label. On the label was written a number and grid reference. An artefact register was also opened in which number, grid reference, description and date of finding were recorded. For example, the very first artefact raised by the expedition was no. 1, F4-8, a copper nail, on 31 January 1986.

Every artefact was then photographed. Sometimes, in the case of a complex shape several pictures were taken. Each picture clearly showed the artefact label, together with a section of measuring tape to give an indication of relative size.

Charlie's next idea was ingenious. I had obtained copies of the plans of the *Birkenhead* from the National Maritime Museum and Charlie scaled these to his plan scale, photocopying and then cutting the copy into the three fragments of the wreck. Laying these on top of his wreck drawing, we could get an idea of precisely where each artefact was found. Some of the plans are shown at pages 2 and 3. The value of this overlay method was shown when we found a crystal tumbler base, the top of the glass gone but the letters C.P. clearly but crudely engraved on its bottom. Who was C.P.? I checked the list of soldiers' names and found one Charles Prince, but he was unranked and would not have been in the stern area which was reserved for officers, the women and children. The mystery was solved by the plan. The crystal tumbler base, no. 38, G5-4, found on 5 February 1986 was in the commander's pantry. The very next day we found another similar base, unfortunately also broken but engraved C.P., also in square G5-4. It received the identification no. 45, G5-4, crystal tumbler base (C.P.), 6/2/86.

It was important that the artefacts be preserved. Glass was no problem, but copper, brass, iron, wood and leather exposed to sea water for over a century rapidly deteriorate when exposed to air again and allowed to dry out. Large plastic baths filled with sea water were kept on board the *Adventurer* for immediate first-aid treatment of all the artefacts. That evening, on return to shore, the sea water would be replaced with fresh water as a primary desalination procedure. Some artefacts would have to be kept in their baths for years, the water being regularly changed to slowly leach the sodium chloride and other sea salts from the wood. Sodium sesquicarbonate would be added to the copper-containing finds to retard the development of acid chlorides which would attack the copper on exposure to atmospheric oxygen, the so-called bronze disease.

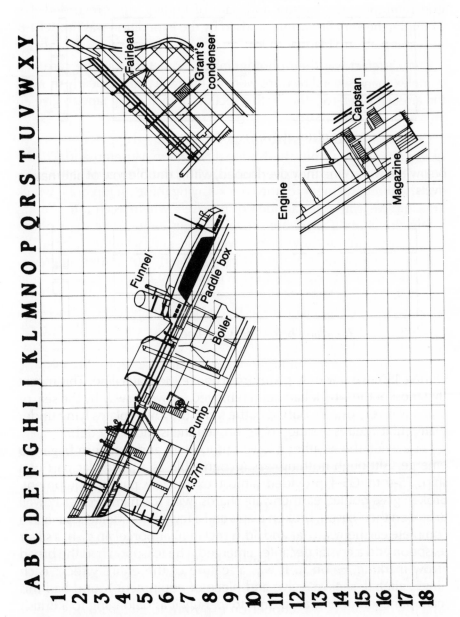

Scattering of the wreck under water

Everything at the wreck site was buried in sand, with broken plates from the hull, ribbing and rocks all sandwiched together and compressed. The plates were an indication of level in the *Birkenhead*. Above the water-line they were butt-jointed with an internal iron strap and two rows of evenly spaced rivets.

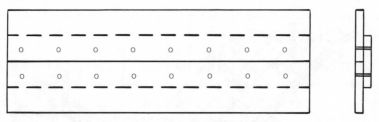

The plates above the water-line

Below the water-line they overlapped, with a double row of alternating rivets.

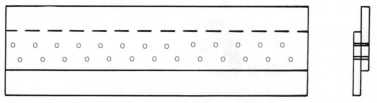

The plates below the water-line

During 1986 we saw only plates from above the water-line. This meant that most of the wreck had been removed or swept away by the sea, or that it was very deeply buried in the sand, the lower plates lying under many cubic metres of sand, rocks, broken shells and other debris.

For a week the weather allowed us to work and a pattern began to emerge. Although nothing was recognisable as a particular part of a ship, F5-4 to G5-4 provided almost exclusively pantry equipment. Broken glass bottles, earthenware shards (with the name Potter Powell Bristol on their bases), broken plates and a few intact artefacts, such as a complete earthenware jar and lid, a rectangular porcelain dish, a silver teaspoon and a crystal decanter emerged. The teaspoon had the broad arrow marking $\rightarrow$ on it. It was a feature of the entire wreck: each hinge, gimbal, sheave, valve and piece of equipment found had this mark punched or engraved on it to identify it as belonging to a British government vessel.

A pewter syringe, a brass toilet bowl (corroded, dented and covered with barnacles and calcific deposits), a broken porthole, a musket-ball mould, a button of the 12th Lancers, a square ink bottle, wooden handles – gradually our collection grew and the position of each artefact was plotted on the developing plan.

On 9 February the sea and the weather closed on us. For six days we were landlocked and we took the time to explore the facilities of Gansbaai and its environs.

A few kilometres north of Gansbaai is a natural cave with mineral pools and gushing springs that flow into the sea. It is called Die Kelders. Sited high above the caves is Die Kelders Hotel which, some years ago, featured in a television series in which it was called the Suidepunt Hotel. The red corrugated roof of Die Kelders still bears the faded name Suidepunt as a proud reminder of its starring days. It has an excellent dining room and, important from our point of view, a half-size snooker table. Rainy and windy days passed amid excited shouts over shots just missed and impossible balls sunk.

Eventually the weather cleared and after a week of mischief the whole team was more than keen to begin diving again. The area G5-4 of a metre square had been the object of a week's work before the weather turned. F5 was now examined.

Dressed in their hot-water suits, a pair of divers breathing from the surface air supply via their long umbilical hoses worked for 80 minutes. As they surfaced they were rapidly recompressed and the next pair dived. For ten hours a day the diving proceeded, one team below and another in the chamber. Area F5-1 to F5-6 once more yielded porcelain, pottery and glass, together with seven silver spoons and a pair of silver sugar tongs. These were imbedded in dense black conglomerate. A large section of hull plating underlay the whole area, buried in sand. Three days were spent clearing the sand from this area with a hydrauli-

Fork and two dessert spoons

cally powered blower. The blower sucked water in from the side and a central fan blew it out again, creating a powerful thrust which smoothly blew away any sand in its path. One diver controlled the force and direction of the water from the blower, aiming it so that the surface sand could be lifted and removed by the current, while the other examined the area by hand. More and more conglomerate, a hard black combination of oxides of iron, sand, marine organisms and precipitated minerals, appeared. The divers began to suffer. It was very laborious chipping away at the conglomerate with chisels and lifting portions with a crowbar, only to find that a large beam of decayed iron was imbedded in the black area.

Tired from a long dive, the divers would surface to be greeted by the rubicund flat backside of the *Adventurer*, rising and slapping back into the water. To assist them, a metal ladder had been built, which hooked on to the stern railing and dipped down into the sea. As the *Adventurer* raised her stern into the air, the ladder rose high out of the water before returning with speed. The two lower ends forked down into the sea like a barbeque prong. To avoid being spiked, the divers had to wait for the ladder to drop, swim for it in the lull before the next rise, grab it and be hauled clean out of the water with the following lift. Timing was everything. On one occasion, Pierre fumbled for an instant. A smashed rib and a broken front tooth was his punishment. This was to cause him a great deal of pain, but he continued to work.

Muscle was needed. In order to continue working in the area, the heavy decayed mass of hull plate and ribbing imbedded in concrete-like conglomerate had to be lifted and shifted. We built a series of slings of heavy steel rope about 3 m long with a loop spliced at each end. The divers would attempt to insinuate the sling under the plate and then attach the looped ends to the end of the winch cable of the *Causeway Adventurer*. The winch would then lift the plate off the work site.

A sling was fitted near one end of the plate, shackled to the winch cable and slowly the huge winch drum took up the slack. As the *Adventurer* rose on her next rump-exposing lift, the winch cable yanked tight. Clouds of black water rose at the bottom and the divers, a discreet distance away, scuttled as visibility declined to zero. The plate trembled. Then, with a loud bang, the sling broke. The winch cable suddenly went slack, metre after metre of cable returning from the sea and dropping to the deck.

We decided that we needed something to compensate for the pitching of the stern, something with elastic properties as well as strength. Clive disappeared into the hold and emerged with a wrist-thick white nylon rope. We would attach this between the sling and the winch cable. Confident that we had solved the problem, we set to work.

Fascinated, the two working divers watched as the nylon rope took the strain. Lengthening and thinning, the rope began to disappear towards the surface. Then, with a grinding roar, a section of plate broke off and moved. Total darkness again covered the entire area as billowing whorls of blackened water spewed over the wreck. Minutes of waiting followed while the current carried the darkness away, exposing the opened area. There was more plate underneath.

Concertina-like, the hull had collapsed layer upon layer as the *Birkenhead* had disintegrated. Incredibly, however, intact porcelain and a tiny Royal Doulton jug depicting a hunting scene had survived the collapse in the small sand-filled crevices between the rotting plates. We were both disheartened and encouraged. It was going to be backbreaking work but we had a method that worked, or so we thought. The winch cable was slung over the large pulley wheel at the apex of the A-frame that was to have launched the bell. We could not use the bell, but the frame allowed us to exert a pull over the stern and our decompression chambers.

With the next pull the nylon rope stretched impossibly and snapped. The heavy winch cable suddenly snarled back on to the deck of the *Adventurer,* looping wire that had everyone scurrying for safety. It slipped off the pulley wheel at the top of the frame which began a high-pitched screaming spin.

The force that the cable had taken was measured at an incredible 80 tons. The workshop which built our A-frame had boasted that it would easily take 50 tons. Without budging or flexing it had taken much more but we were not at all enthusiastic to repeat the test.

It was obvious that we could not simply use the power of the winch to lift long lengths of rivetted plating. We would continue to snap slings as fast as we made them. The packed masses of plating and iron beams had to be cut to convenient sizes or holes drilled in the plating to permit easier lifting. We used a Broco torch, a device that passes oxygen through a tube containing magnesium wires. Electrically sparking the end of the tube under water started a fierce flame that cut through iron with sizzling ease and a boil of surrounding water.

The engines and boilers of the *Birkenhead* were mounted in a single cavernous compartment 21 m long, extending from the bottom bilge plates right up to the top deck and occupying the entire middle third of the vessel. The coal bunkers were sited on both sides of this chamber and extended along its length at the lower deck level. These were filled with an additional 350 tons of coal when the troopship anchored at

Simon's Bay. When the *Birkenhead* broke, tons of coal had spilled out of her bunkers, tumbling and scattering over the wreck site. Some was buried in the sand, some covered by hull plate as it crumpled and collapsed over the years, and the rest stayed in the conglomerating bins.

Working near a coal bunker to one side of the destroyed boilers one day, Italo was busily cutting through a plate. Underneath the plate was coal which began to warm up with the intense heat from the torch. Eventually it became red-hot and the stage was set for the formation of combustible gases. The presence of oxygen and fire did the rest. The coal exploded. A pressure wave suddenly hurled Italo from his position. Buffeted backwards, his arms and legs akimbo and his umbilical hose dragging through the liquid resistance of the sea, he landed unconscious in the sand several metres away. He recovered to find himself on his back, uninjured and his air supply still firmly gripped in his mouth.

A daily discussion was held on the bridge where we kept the plans of the *Birkenhead*. With each new item of information, each new find, we would pore over the copies, looking at deck plan after deck plan to identify exactly where we were on the wreck. Arguments and sometimes tempers flared but the *Birkenhead* remained inscrutable. We had much more to do before any real answers were to be had. Many more dives were needed.

The divers working on the wreck were tendered by two men on the stern railing of the tug. Each diver had one man constantly holding his air line, taking up slack and giving more hose as the diver moved. Any problem on the dive could be signalled to the surface by a system of tugs on the hose. One tug meant 'Attention!', two tugs 'Down, or slack off', and so on. Similarly, if the weather turned bad, which it could do within minutes, the diver could be signalled to commence his ascent immediately. We learnt to judge the sea. From far away, the foam-flecked crests of agitated swells, wind-swept like the flying manes of white horses, could be seen approaching. With someone's warning, 'Here comes the cavalry', the men on air line duty would get ready to abort the dive.

Observing the sea is an art. When I first arrived at Gansbaai, I marvelled at the ability of the Cape half of the team to assess the water. Standing on the shore they would take one look at the sea and say, 'It's OK' or, 'Today's a washout.' Peering at the surface of the sea with inland eyes I could never see how they knew. It always looked fine to me unless there was an obvious gale blowing. After months I began to get the idea. Swells that are metres high look like ripples from the shore. The frequency of swells, their presence or absence in key areas, the direction and force of the wind, the colour of the water, the phase of the moon and the time of the year are all important indicators. Somehow one becomes attuned to these things and suddenly it all makes sense. Eventually I, too, could squint at the sea with sage eyes and make judgements.

The problem was standing on the stern of the heaving *Adventurer*. Every so often, a particular sequence of swells would set up an oscillating up-and-down rhythm in the movement of the tug and we learnt to scramble when a mammoth descent was due. A wall of water would climb over the stern, totally covering the wailing men on tender duty while the rest of the divers and crew shrieked with laughter, knowing that their turn would come. On one fine day I was facing the bows midway up the stern deck when a behemoth roared over the stern. Suddenly waist deep in water, I was swept up the deck, dunked onto the planks and rolled on to my belly.

Sitting high up in the bridge, Clive Gibson buried his face in his arms as his shoulders shook with mirth. Just before I became submerged, I saw the purpling face of Stein, his open mouth framing little irregular teeth in preparation for a titanic guffaw. As I gathered up myself, my wits and what was left of my dignity, I saw the men on the stern rail clutching for dear life, totally drenched and spitting sea water, but still holding the umbilicals to the divers.

Limited by the conglomerate and plating, work was continuing 2 m further astern on the wreck, in the F4-7, F5-1, E4-9 and E5-3 sections, a total area of 2 m by 2 m. Some glass with an etched crown and anchor emerged together with a porcelain saucer and jug shards. Then military artefacts began to appear. On 17 February 1986 a leather pouch filled with lead shot, several badly corroded double rifle barrels, and a sword scabbard were eased from their heavy covering of conglomerate. Although the sword had long disappeared, the leather of the scabbard was in excellent condition, still pliable despite its long immersion. As if the divers had passed through a door, the conglomerate then released a brass doorknob and a brass keyhole cover. A bowl shard with an anchor and the words 'Flora B & T' was followed by shoes – men's shoes, square-tipped and remarkably narrow and long; ladies' shoes; a little shoe, and fragments of shoes, almost all intact and soft-leathered. We were in a store. A leather harness with buckles and clips, wooden implement handles, a hairbrush handle, a copper birdshot pouch, brass hasps and a weight, a cutthroat razor, knife handles, a bottle with a ground glass stopper, and then spoons. Four silver spoons, all bent and blackened, a brass spoon and two pieces of a silver pot were gently chipped from their black bed of conglomerate. A few more glass stoppers, a glass bottle, some buttons and an earthenware jug were found and then again immovable hull plate concreted in black.

Came 26 February, the anniversary of the sinking of the *Birkenhead*. It was 134 years to the day since she sank, but the sea was angry and would not let us near her. Waves smashed against the concrete walls of the little harbour, sending water soaring over the pier and causing chaos among the hurriedly moored fishing boats. They bumped and ground against each other, mooring lines snapped, and yelling fishermen struggled with heavy ropes to regain control and limit the damage.

The next day dawned bright and clear and the sea was flat. We had invited Dr Chris Loedolff and Jalmar Rudner from the National Monuments Council to come and watch us work that day and were pleased that the elements favoured the visit. We were due to meet only around midday, so early in the morning we travelled as usual in *Seaker* to the *Adventurer*, did our morning leap and made for the rock.

The well established sequence of diving and decompressing slid smoothly into motion again. My job was to operate the chambers to ensure that the divers were correctly pressurised and decompressed for the required time, and to monitor the air supply and compressors. It was a glorious day, the sea was clear and blue and the wind just a cool breeze. Right at the top of the mast the anemometer idly turned, speeding up a little from time to time as a vagrant gust filled its cups.

Surfacing from his dive, Pierre Joubert, his swarthy face a little puffy from the long immersion, climbed the ladder and placed his blue gloves on the deck. Without a word he sat down as quick hands stripped off his suit and equipment before he entered the lock for recompression. As Pierre and his diving partner, Konrad, transferred into the main chamber, I heard them laughing over the intercom and then a yell from Charlie on the deck. He had picked up Pierre's gloves and, feeling a weight in one of them, had emptied the glove on to the wooden planking of the deck.

A lead musket ball rolled out and then gold sovereigns, sixteen glinting, gleaming, shining discs that spun and flashed in the sun and came to rest. Everyone rushed to Charlie. His expression a mixture of dazed disbelief and a dawning smile, he held them out for all to see. George III, George IV, William IV, and Victoria, profiles of British Majesty and symbols of her wealth. The day after the anniversary of her demise, the *Birkenhead* had presented us with gold. I have rarely witnessed such an exhibition of prancing jubilation.

We all crowded into the little control cabin and the intercom buzzed as Pierre tried to explain exactly where he had discovered the coins. He

Reverse of George IV with Pistrucci design of St George on charger

As above

Obverse of George IV

Reverse of William IV

Obverse of William IV

Victoria

Sovereigns, obverse

Sovereigns, reverse

84

could not leave the chamber for another forty minutes and the next team was aching to dive.

As Italo and Alan prepared for their dive there was a sense of tense expectancy on board. Would they find any more coins?

Charlie and I left the *Adventurer* in *Seaker* to call for Chris and Jalmar at Gansbaai. We were as excited as little children. Our adventure and expedition was really working! As a boy I had read tales of high excitement at sea and now I was actually involved in a real story. With the wind blowing in my face as we sped across the bay, I experienced a joy in living and a surge of vitality. Looking at Charlie I saw he was in accord. He, too, was experiencing the heart-thumping adrenalin-fired euphoria, faster and faster we flew across the water, our combined laughter trailing behind us with the spray in the wake of *Seaker's* screaming engines.

Cooling our enthusiasm to a level of only moderate mania, we greeted our guests who showed remarkable diplomacy on being confronted with inane grins on a sunny day. We returned to the *Adventurer* at a much more sedate pace and with more than a little pride showed Chris and Jalmar our work, our equipment and technology, the neatly labelled and catalogued artefacts and Charlie's grid drawings. Discussing and explaining, we waited for Italo and Alan to surface. They had found one more sovereign. As pair after pair of divers followed, the tension mounted but no more coins were found that day.

Our visitors had certainly witnessed an afternoon of high excitement, and when Chris and Jalmar returned to shore they surely carried with them an unforgettable memory of their day at sea.

All eyes were on Pierre when he dived the next day.

Returning to the narrow space between the decaying iron ribs he worked into the sand, clearing and sifting very carefully. With a giant grin that threatened to split his face he surfaced and once more placed a blue glove on the wooden deck. Seven sovereigns beamed in the sun. In all, 27 sovereigns and a badly worn shilling were recovered as the diving teams tried to emulate 'Fingers' Joubert's example.

Two days later the news broke in the Sunday papers. Not only did we make the front page complete with full-colour photographs once again, but we were posted on billboards outside every news outlet in the country: 'GOLD STRIKE!' This was the trigger that started a new attack on our work.

The coins we had found were not enough to confirm that the *Birkenhead* was indeed carrying a pay packet to Algoa Bay. Even in those days it was expensive to be an officer and a gentleman. Rank could be obtained by purchase and to become an ensign in the Dragoons cost £840, while the rank of lieutenant-colonel could be had for £6 175. As an example, Alexander Seton in overall charge of the troops had purchased his second and first lieutenancy, been promoted to captain in the 74th Highlanders without purchase, and had purchased his major's rank for £4 575 in 1850. While on the *Birkenhead* he had received his rank of lieutenant-colonel without purchase. It was highly probable that the sovereigns belonged to an officer quartered in the stern.

The professional archaeologists insisted on a moratorium on all new permits. This did not last very long and did not affect us. There was also a change in wreck legislation which had long been in the pipeline. Conditions were made more strict and although our permit had been issued prior to that, our work complied with these conditions. There was a new flurry of exchanges between the South African and British governments, both again claiming ownership of the wreck. The coins were put into bond in a bank vault pending the outcome of negotiations between the British Ministry of Defence and our Department of Foreign Affairs, and the salvage continued.

Plates and bedrock now blocked the areas we had examined. As massive plate removal would irrevocably change the whole aspect of the wreck as it lay, we decided to leave the area and examine the surrounding grid squares until plate was again reached. Only then would plating be lifted and the next layer assessed. We moved to the H to J, 6 to 8 grid sections. This corresponded to the engine-room spares area, the mess area, carpenter's room, gunner's room, provisions stores, and army officers' rooms at different levels on the *Birkenhead*. It was also the area where the large pump was housed, the pump that had caused the death of sixty men vainly striving to keep the broken *Birkenhead* afloat. The artefacts found would give us an indication of level, whether we were on the upper deck, main deck or in the lower decks.

More shoes, shot, a wine bottle, pieces of uniform with buttons attached and brass emerged. The uniform pieces were cotton, elasticised with the thin thread-like brown elastic that used to be popular on ladies' two-ways in the 1950s. The shreds were too small to determine any rank or regiment but the buttons were pewter, indicating an unranked uniform. Buttons located in the officers' area on the *Birkenhead* were brass, frequently gold-plated, whereas the buttons found in the bows and forward sections where the troops were quartered were made of pewter.

The brass comprised oil lamp parts, hinges, locks, cupboard handles,

Brass hasp

a key, a section of a hasp, and a magnificent pair of calipers beautifully engraved and designed to measure the bore of large guns and cannon. We were in the area of Gunner Archbold's room on the main deck, starboard side.

We never found the ship's pump that cost the lives of all those men. The story in Gansbaai has it that a Cape Town diver, thinking it was an engine, removed it from the wreck and sold it for its scrap brass value. It apparently stood on the pier at the harbour for weeks before being taken away and destroyed.

Disaster struck after we had been working for four weeks. We had just changed to a new oxygen bank. Italo and Malcolm were both in the decompression chamber, inhaling the oxygen so vital for their decompression schedule. Within the systems control room and listening through my earphones, I heard Italo ask Malcolm, 'Does your oxygen taste funny?'

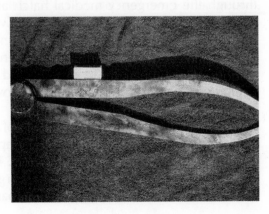

Brass calipers for measuring the calibre of cannons

'No,' said Malcolm, 'what's the matter?'

Italo removed his oxygen mask. Malcolm stared at Italo's face. His mouth, nose and lips, which had been covered by the mask, were a dirty brown. Italo opened his mouth. His tongue and cheeks were also stained.

'Water and rust must have gotten into the system,' muttered Italo, and took a tentative sniff from his mask.

Then both of them started choking and spluttering as acrid brown liquid bubbled from the breathing system.

'Allan!' they yelled.

Shutting off the oxygen control valve on the main console, I rushed to the chamber and closed the oxygen inlet valve mounted directly on the shell. Within the chamber, Italo closed the internal shell valve. The chamber was now totally isolated from its oxygen supply. I noted the time. Both men were now breathing pressurised chamber air. This meant they were going to start absorbing nitrogen again.

With the help of Konrad I began dismantling the alloy pipes behind the console which supplied the chamber. We found them to be filled with filthy pungent liquid. But where could it have come from? The system was completely sealed, with valve after valve backing up its integrity. There was only one possibility – our bank of medical oxygen was contaminated. Hurriedly we disconnected the hose to the bank. Brown fluid dribbled from the hose. We opened the oxygen manifold tap. A gush of foul liquid sprayed from the pressurised oxygen cylinders. We ran to the next bank, still bearing the manufacturer's seal. Brown fluid sprayed out. Aghast, we checked yet another bank. It was clean. Using our high-pressure air banks, we blasted air through all the external valving and piping of the oxygen supply system, blowing until no more liquid vented out.

Meanwhile, tools and cloths had been passed into the chamber through the emergency medical hatch and Italo and Malcolm were stripping and cleaning their masks and valves.

Recoupling the system and connecting it to the clean bank, we passed the oxygen through our percentage analyser. It was pure. Valves were reopened, masks replaced and the decompression schedule amended. Nearly two hours later the brown-faced Italo and Malcolm emerged, both intact and very angry.

We only had one more usable bank of oxygen. The cylinders were all to be replaced later by a stunned and apologetic gas company, but a great deal of valuable time had been lost. The cylinders had apparently been contaminated with cleaning detergent. For some inexplicable reason, this had been left in most of our banks before they were filled.

Hip-flask with lid removed

Pocket-knife, letter opener and cutthroat razor

Porthole

Shard ('Flora B & T')

Lotion bottle

Fragments of porcelain
showing sheep, men and
castle

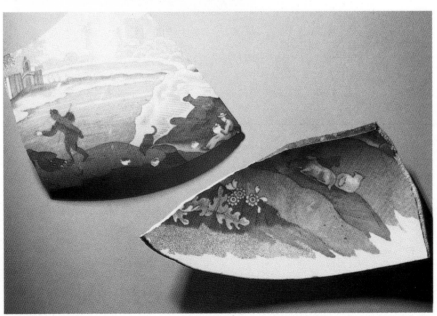

ABOVE: *Porcelain dish and lid showing a boat approaching a rock*

LEFT: *A pot whose three pieces – lid and two large fragments – were recovered on three separate occasions and then pieced together*

BELOW: *Shard of pottery with statue of rider on rearing charger and ship; glass fragment with anchor and VR (Victoria Regina)*

The *Adventurer* was now needed elsewhere. Stowing all our equipment, we returned to Cape Town for a change of vessels. We had been working on site for a month. Waiting for us at Table Bay harbour was the Pentow Marine vessel, the *Reunion* captained by the salty and fiery Ernie Fitzgerald. We had gained much experience in handling our heavy equipment. It took one day to transfer and relocate ourselves on the *Reunion*. Our chambers were too large and heavy to place on the *Reunion*, but a small chamber, perfectly adequate for our needs and supplied by South African Diving Services, was already welded on board. Newly painted and maintained, it contrasted sharply with the already worn appearance of our machinery, beaten and sprayed by the rough seas.

Much smaller than the *Adventurer*, the *Reunion* had one huge advantage. We could now moor with our bows into the current and still dive over the flat stern deck. There would be no more thumping and crashing. The vessel could also enter Gansbaai harbour every night and we would be able to board her directly at the quay every morning, so the morning leaps were a thing of the past. The cramped deck space and tiny galley were more than adequately compensated for.

With flags flying and the newly polished ship's bell in position next to the entrance to the bridge, Ernie set course from Cape Town for the *Birkenhead* the next night. When we rounded Cape Point many of the crew and those of our group aboard became violently seasick with the much quicker movement of the *Reunion*. We crossed False Bay and berthed at Gansbaai the following day.

The next morning we all packed into the bridge to watch Ernie's technique and approach to the rock. Blocking his passage, getting in his way, sitting on his control buttons, we rapidly drove him mad and received the full brunt of his volatile nature. Changing our behaviour to suit the confines of a much smaller vessel was necessary.

With the *Reunion* we used a four-point mooring. Cutting his bow anchor chain, Ernie shackled a metal buoy to the free end, and over it went to form a north mooring point.

A rubber dinghy on the deck of the *Reunion* was to be used to haul the much lighter mooring ropes to the four buoys each day. No longer did Charlie and Mike have to travel to the rock in *Seaker* to await the arrival of the diving boat.

The break over the rock was now very close. We still had our stern over the stern of the *Birkenhead*, but instead of pointing away from the rock towards land, our bows faced south into the current and the sea. Like a cradle, we rocked gently in the swell. What a difference from the crashing, banging ride on the *Adventurer*!

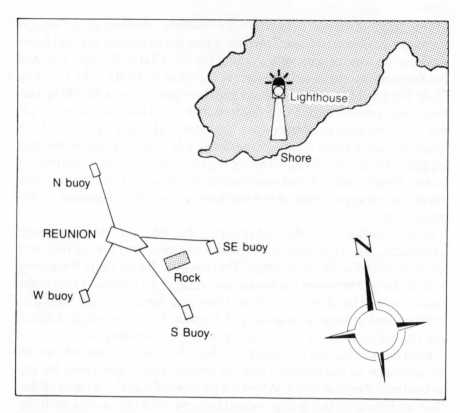

Measurements of the wreck were taken almost every day. On the big tug we had made a 'triangulation ring' consisting of a metal circle with an external diameter of exactly 3 600 mm. In the centre of the ring a stainless-steel indicator arm pivoted, moving over the edge which was graduated, each 10-mm mark representing one degree of arc. The ring was fixed to a sturdy tripod and placed at a determined point, such as the tiller arm on the stern. A glass-fibre tape attached to the end of the indicator measured the distance to any given second point and the edge markings showed the angle. The method required two people, one to read off the angle and the other to swim to the second point and read off the distance. Each diver had a sanded perspex sheet upon which he wrote his readings in pencil.

For example:	DIVER 1	DIVER 2
	1. 124 deg.	Front-end cannon 17,45 m
	2. 126 deg.	Back-end cannon 16,37 m

The method worked but required synchronisation. If the divers managed to get their readings out of phase, the information was useless. With the poor visibility on the *Birkenhead*, the second diver was often out of sight of the first and a mistake in sequence was easy. If this happened, the second diver had to swim backward and forward to the ring too often. On the surface, Charlie would add the angled measurements to scale on his drawing.

Jimmy Herbert, at the time also a member of the Aqua diving team, was busy with a course in archaeology. One weekend he brought a plastic sextant which could be used under water to the site. The angles between objects could be measured with the sextant and if we knew the length of one side of any triangle, the others could be plotted. The water at the wreck is gloomy, however, and objects more than a few metres away are vague. Thus, the sextant was not practical.

Charlie then began multiple triangulations. From a fixed point, he directly measured the distance to a series of objects and wrote them down. He then measured the distances from a second point to the same objects and noted these. The known distance between the first and second points gave a whole group of triangles and a rapid method of underwater plotting. The orientation of the various broken portions of the wreck began to become clear. A cannon thought to face forward, actually faced more inward and the lie between the two cannons, the engine spares and the boiler emerged. On days when the ship was unable to stay on site, a ski-boat frequently could, and dives on scuba were then done in order to measure and plot.

It was nearly mid-March and dawn was getting later and later. We left for the *Birkenhead* at 07h00, having breakfast *en route*.

The exploration continued. We moved to the bow section, measuring and correlating. The position of Grant's condenser was mapped, the capstan lying on the rock was noted, the fairleads of the bows, the anchors and chain, the engine of the troopship, all were plotted and examined. From the R to V, 8 to 9 area in which the troops had slept, brass rifle side-plates, trigger guards, buckles, clips and pewter buttons emerged. A skylight lens was found, a rectangular piece of glass, with one surface moulded into a tetrahedral prism. It had a brass plate with which it had been fixed to the roof of the deck to admit and dissipate light. In the J7 section, corresponding to the baggage room, we had a splendid find. A brass nameplate, still attached to a backing piece of leather and elegantly engraved, surfaced on 14 March. It read 'G.A. Lucas Esq.' This was Ensign Lucas of the 73rd Foot, destined to survive the disaster and become Chief Magistrate of Natal, the man who had initiated the very first *Birkenhead* syndicate. Sadly, no more pertaining to him was found.

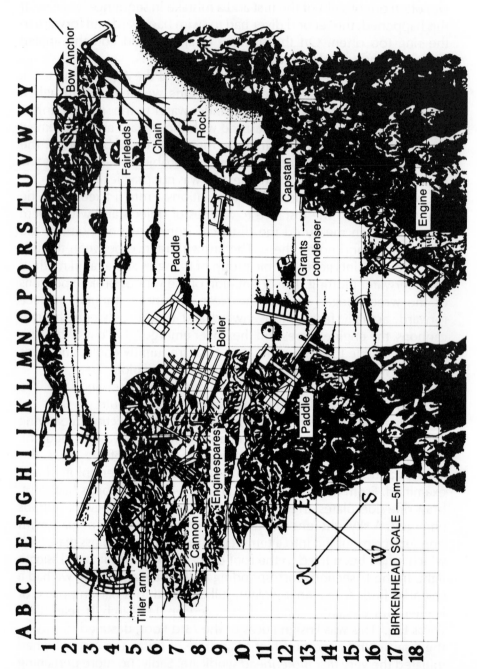

Drawing of the lie of the wreck

There were just seven more diving days in the next three weeks. The weather was worsening, the currents were becoming stronger and our equipment was badly in need of maintenance. Italo, with his genius for repair and rigging, was hard pressed to keep the tired and leaking hot-water machine going and the compressors needed attention. The impatient and sorely tried families of the married divers had become weary of having to cope with the normal world, pay the bills and look after the home, the children and their schooling while the gentleman of the house followed his dream.

The *Reunion* had developed trouble with one of her engines and repairs could be done only in Cape Town. It was time to leave and renew.

Strife, Vulcan and Wine

The *Government Gazette* of 2 April 1986 spelled out the amendments to the War Graves and National Monuments Act. A permit was now a requirement for work on any wreck older than 50 years. Intent to salvage had to be published in the *Government Gazette* before any permit could be validated. Any person not complying with the new law faced a very stiff fine or jail sentence.

The battle had recommenced between archaeologists and salvage divers, with our work at the heart of the attack. The arena was the news media. It was stated that all work on vessels should be left to marine archaeologists, that any salvage should follow the procedures of a land dig, and that theses and questions should be formulated in advance before any work was started. The salvage would then be used to confirm or refute the objectives.

On 14 March an underwater science symposium was held at the University of Cape Town, during which the salvage of historic wrecks, the current legislation, the National Monuments Council and our work on the *Birkenhead* were criticised. Neither the NMC nor we were invited to this symposium to answer the critics or discuss our work.

Three days later a letter appeared in the *Cape Times* deploring the inability of the NMC to control salvage work and questioning our motives, ability and trustworthiness. The letter cited the case of a 'mustard jar' which we had recovered, still corked, and which we had reportedly opened 'to see what was inside'. It continued that 'no archaeological scientist would open a jar to expose the contents to the air without sampling under controlled circumstances in a laboratory. The entire operation has been strictly one of legalised mining of a part of South Africa's cultural heritage'.

It is a pity that the accuracy of reports in the Sunday press was not questioned. We had recovered several jars, still intact, and none had ever been opened. The mustard pot had opened itself. Putrefaction had occurred during the 134 years of deep submersion. Gases generated by this process had been kept in solution by the high surrounding water pressure. At the surface, however, the mustard pot was exposed to only one atmosphere of pressure. With the drop in ambient pressure, bubbles began to develop within the jar. Hydrogen sulphide and other gases of putrefaction left their dissolved state and, boiling free in their gas form, dislodged the cork and spewed the contents from the jar. The mustard pot was experiencing a severe case of the bends! A sample of the mustard was kept for subsequent analysis, which established that it had a pH of 1,7 due to the acid hydrogen sulphide. It was English mustard as traces of the glucoside sinalbin were found. Black mustard, more favoured in Europe, contains the glucoside sinigrin. No trace of this was detected.

The problem was how to handle putrescent organic material without allowing it to decompress explosively. It could not simply be rapidly repressurised in a chamber and then decompressed as one would do with a nitrogen-laden diver. His dissolved gases are absorbed from outside, from his air supply, and are returned to the atmosphere with each exhaled breath during decompression. The gases in our pot were not absorbed from without, but were generated inside the container as the mustard slowly rotted. Its thick waxed cork was impervious to gases. They would have diffused into the sea along a concentration gradient if it were porous. Decompressing the pot through its cork would not have worked.

The antagonism then went on the air in Radio Today, where the attack on the NMC and us was continued. The SABC approached Chris Loedolff, Director of the NMC, who pointed out that the NMC consulted widely before issuing a permit, and that our operation was the best planned and best equipped one they had approved.

While the media revelled in all the controversy, the salvage was raised in the South African Parliament. Questions on the salvage, our permit and ownership were put to the Minister of National Education by a member of the Opposition. Chris Loedolff in his capacity as Director of the NMC supplied the answers.

The artefacts found, nearly 300 in number, had been transferred to Cape Town, still in their protective baths. The Cultural History Museum was notified and invited to examine them as it was to their museum that many would ultimately be donated. Our reports, artefact register and drawings were given to the NMC, and research into the *Birkenhead* continued while we waited for the next season of diving.

The question of the figurehead of the *Birkenhead* was the subject of much speculation in our discussions. It was an effigy of Vulcan, the god of fire and patron of metalworkers. He had a hammer in one hand and a thunderbolt in the other. As the arms were outstretched, we reasoned that it could have been made of metal, hopefully brass, as wooden arms would be liable to break. The wooden figureheads we had previously seen had their arms at their sides for increased strength. As the *Birkenhead* was one of the early metal-hulled ships, we hoped that we would be able to locate a metal Vulcan. I wrote to David Bevan who went to enormous lengths to solve the question. Writing back to me he said:

I have spoken to a great many people about the figurehead, including a fellow named Frank Lindstrom who works for Cammell Laird (Shipbuilders) Ltd. at the City of Birkenhead. It appears that in years past all the figureheads for the ships they built were put out to contract with small local firms. They no longer have records going back to 1852, so he cannot give me the name of the company who made our particular figurehead. However, I have got both the Town Hall at Birkenhead and the local museum there searching through their records for all the names and addresses of local firms who would have made figureheads in the mid-nineteenth century. When I have this data I will follow it through from there.

I also went to the National Maritime Museum at Greenwich and I've been to the Naval Museum at Portsmouth. I have spoken to experts at both places regarding figureheads and it is their considered opinion that Vulcan would have been made totally of wood. It seems that whatever shape the various figureheads took, they seldom lasted the life of the ship and were frequently replaced. On the Cutty Sark at Greenwich they have a fine collection of figureheads, many of which have arms outstretched and they are all made totally of wood. There was an old 'sea-salt' working on the Cutty Sark and I spoke to him for ages about the Birkenhead and he too was of the opinion that there would have been no metal on Vulcan.

We had to accept that Vulcan had in all probability been wooden and that meant that he was gone forever. Sited on the prow of the *Birkenhead*, he would have been involved in the impact zone when the ship hit the rock. What was left after the impact would have been demolished by the wave, rock and currents.

In September 1986 I had the privilege of meeting David Molyneux-Berry, the authority on vinology at Sothebys. An auction of rare wines was being held by the Gilbey group in Johannesburg. They had heard that we had located some wine bottles. Two of the bottles were rushed up from our artefact store in Cape Town and at my home one Saturday I witnessed a master in action. He immediately identified one of the bottles as one of the early moulded bottles made by Ricketts in Bristol. There was no name on the bottle, but during the next expedition we were to find a broken wine bottle base with the moulded words 'Ricketts Bristol' upon it.

Mr Molyneux-Berry identified the second bottle as a blown Constantia bottle, which meant that the *Birkenhead* had taken on Constantia wines when she anchored in Simon's Bay before leaving for Algoa Bay and her end. We then discussed the methods to be used in determining the contents of the bottles, aseptic techniques and chemical tests. The area where the wine bottles were found was well marked as many other bottles were expected to emerge as the salvage proceeded.

Another fascinating fact was that the wines on the *Birkenhead* pre-dated the *Phylloxera* aphid which was inadvertently imported from California into the European wine areas in the early 1860s. This pest attacked the roots of the vines and wiped out nearly two million acres of French vines and completely destroyed the entire wine industry of Madeira. Resistant roots were then imported form California and all the later Burgundies and Madeiras, among others, were produced from grafts on to these roots. This holds true to this day.

What were the chances of the wines on the *Birkenhead* having survived over a century of immersion in sea water? The temperature at the bottom was conducive to survival but, in Mr Molyneux-Berry's experience, few wines have survived exposure to sea water. The cork is not impervious to the gradual passage of water, minerals and marine bacteria, and contamination inevitably occurs. This unfortunately turned out to be true. An uncontaminated bottle of wine off HMS *Birkenhead* would have been enormously valuable.

The National Monuments Council invited us to present a talk on the *Birkenhead* at a symposium on maritime archaeology to be held at the Cultural History Museum in Cape Town. It was to be a full day's presentation by a number of people involved in a variety of maritime fields. We were to be given the opportunity to present our work in an official and scientific meeting, where we could show our techniques and progress and our antagonists could state their objections openly and in our presence. I was to present the research and cultural and historical aspects of the salvage, while Charlie Shapiro would discuss the techniques and results of the expedition.

Travelling by air to the Cape, I was filled with excitement at the prospect of presenting my particular obsession, confident that Charlie would acquit himself with his usual thoroughness, but also apprehensive of the onslaught from the archaeological world that I fully expected.

Our talk was scheduled for the afternoon and during lunch I became aware that some of the archaeologists had left. Hypersensitive following the criticism we had endured in the media, I wondered whether we were now going to be blackballed.

The talk featured the political, socio-economic, technological and geographical aspects of the *Birkenhead*. The war in Southern Africa, the famine in Ireland, the iron vessel and an unknown rock – all had combined at one point in time to end the lives of hundreds. Charlie took up the story, taking us forward to the present salvage. As his pictures of the wreck, our techniques, the artefacts and finally the coins lit up the screen I saw that we certainly had the attention of the room. When the lights came on, there was a barrage of questions, real questions and genuine queries. A really gratifying interest was shown without any condemnation or attack. It appeared as if our work was to be regarded as more than a 'mining operation'.

Most importantly, the symposium had shown that salvage divers and scientists could co-exist under the right circumstances. If academic skills can be coupled with physical underwater prowess, the best of both worlds could be had.

It was summer again. Throughout autumn, winter and spring we had earned our separate livelihoods and waited for the next season. Our objective was the systematic search of the wreck, starting at the bows. We had already defined the lie of the wreck and the distribution of most of the many fragments, some made by previous salvors and some by the sea. Hundreds of tons of sand had to be cleared from the site. Plates would have to be exposed, cleared and then lifted. The artefacts found in each area had to be recorded and protected. We were to spend four months on site in 1987 and, as new equipment was ordered and prepared, the familiar excitement of renewing the work was felt.

Birkenhead Revisited

January 1987 saw us once again at Table Bay harbour with the *Reunion* in the lay-up basin. She was being refitted with two brand-new engines and we were cleaning and maintaining our diving equipment in readiness for the months ahead.

It was a reunion on the *Reunion*. Charlie arrived, his curly sun-bleached hair framing his deeply tanned face. With him was Mike, his eyes sparkling behind his spectacles and looking eagerly at the equipment stacked on the dockside. Both had smiles, handshakes and willing arms and backs. André appeared with a new pair of glasses and his hairy grin. Malcolm, his moustache gone but as poised as ever, gazed at us blandly as we greeted him with ribald laughs at his clean appearance. From the bridge of the *Reunion* Ernie peered down at us, his snowy beard a little longer than the previous year. With a beer in his hand he waved us aboard. Joining him, we renewed our friendship and retold last year's jokes.

There were several new members on the team. Konrad Stutterheim was unable to join us again and his place was taken by another diving instructor, Nick Bartlett. He has extensive diving experience in the North Sea and, fearless and impetuous, he brought new strength and spirit to the diving team.

Erik was also absent. He had injured his back and was lying in the Somerset Hospital recovering from spinal surgery. On visiting him there, he greeted us with his flashing smile but his disappointment at being unable to join us was very evident. His replacement was Paul van der Merwe, an NAUI diving instructor who arrived on a monster motorcycle with a roar of power and a black shirt and helmet proclaiming him the captain of the 'Black Baron' diving team. He regaled us with a vast store of jokes, most of which had a genie who granted three wishes.

Ken de Goede, with his cigars, telephone calls, cheery nature and love of beer could not make the season either. In his place was André Steenberg, recently married, very much in love, the youngest of us all

99

and a provincial South African Underwater Union instructor. Now we had two Andrés, André Hartman and André Steenberg. At first they were Big André and Little André, but then Little André mentioned that at school he was called 'Klippies', Afrikaans for little stones. We dubbed him Rocky and then, although his blonde, slight appearance did not even remotely resemble Sylvester Stallone, we renamed him Rambo and so he remained for the whole season.

While the *Reunion* was being refitted in Cape Town, we went to the site of the wreck by ski-boat to check the area once more. Two of the large mooring buoys and Ernie's north buoy were gone. The sea had managed to corrode through nearly 5 cm of steel cable in one year, at least enough for the buoys, tugged by currents and storms, to snap them. The two seven-ton anchors and the heavy chain attached to them, as well as Ernie's bow anchor and chain were at the bottom of the sea. A magnetometer was towed over the area in an attempt to find them but no trace was registered.

A compass search was done in each area. Italo found his chain and anchor almost immediately. They were lying directly in his line of search. André did not use a compass. The feel of the direction of the current on his body was indicator enough for him. Charlie found his too, and once more a trio of marker floats danced, awaiting the *Reunion* so that new buoys and cables could be attached to the submerged chains.

For two weeks we chafed at the bit as the *Reunion*'s engines were installed and tested by the authorities. Her recently painted green deck held two large new mooring buoys, both a bright yellow in bilious contrast. Once more the shining *Reunion* bell was hung and, with her new engines giving a throaty beat and smoke pouring from her funnels, she left for Gansbaai harbour.

We stayed in a house in Gansbaai overlooking Walker Bay. From the balcony we could see the *Reunion* in the harbour, surrounded by blue-hulled fishing vessels with names such as *Blougans* and *Seegans*. Behind them the smoke from the fish factory billowed, producing a scene of picture postcard serenity only belied by the stench. One street away was the cemetery, row after neat row of headstones with the inscriptions all facing away from the sea as if to hide from the waves the names of those who had lived and sometimes died on the water.

Seven of us doubled up in the house and the daily rush for the first hot-water bath, the toilet and the washing machine began. Below the house a large cellar had been converted into a party area with coloured globes, a grill, tables and stools. This was to see many evenings of song and barbeques, with Nick and Malcolm on the guitar, André on the flute, and me hiding my false harmonica notes in the general volume. We even developed a 'Birkenhead song', similar to 'Ver in die Bosveld' and sang and played with huge feeling and choruses of 'Dai-de-dai-dai-dai-daiii-daiii'.

One day, while sitting in the bridge of the Reunion I wrote some words for the song. We never did get to memorise and really sing them, but the mood was there. It went:

> Young men, those who died there
> Four hundred and more
> We must save the women
> Get the children ashore!
>
> Theirs is the honour
> The sea is their grave
> Danger Point is their tombstone
> Overlooking that wave.
>
> Birkenhead was the troopship
> The rock lay in wait
> A crag in the ocean
> So sealing their fate.
>
> We have returned there
> The story to read
> The hull is all broken
> Destroyed by the deed.
>
> She's covered in sand now
> Her soldiers are gone
> Her anchors lie scattered
> Her engines are done.
>
> We'll stretch every sinew
> Our battle we'll wage
> For ours is the honour
> To write the last page.

With André's flute a butterfly flitting in harmony in and out of the theme, and Nick playing both his guitar and harmonica at the same time, I believe the music was really good.

In the relative peace of their room, Charlie and Malcolm had developed an adoration of Foster and Allen, and Irish music from their guitars began to fill the house, while Charlie quietly crooned songs of love and longing.

Ernie had given us a two-way radio which we kept on top of the kitchen fridge. This served as our early morning reveille call. Each day began with Ernie's 'Come on, we haven't got all day', his voice a nasally distorted 'Nah nah nah' over the small crackling speaker. A hasty cup of terrible coffee, and off we were. Ernie later amended his wake-up technique by simply holding his alarm clock next to the microphone. I am invariably an early riser and most mornings, while sitting in the kitchen, I would hear the speaker come alive, then the ratcheting sound of the clock being wound, followed by a shrill ring.

Packing into Charlie's Range Rover, with Nick and sometimes Malcolm jogging to the harbour, we drove to the *Reunion*. Italo arrived separately. He had wisely chosen to live in a different house with his family, so avoiding the utter bedlam of an all-male diving commune.

The *Reunion*'s first task was to replace the missing mooring buoys. The yellow buoys were shackled to the chains on the seabed with long lengths of new steel rope and the marker floats removed. Once more, the rock was encircled and we began to dive again.

A totally unexpected problem immediately presented itself. The particularly savage winter storms that had snapped our mooring lines had also washed thousands of red bait pods down from the rock. Work was begun in the S8 area, which corresponded to the forward galley in the bows. The pods covered everything and removing them was a problem that took weeks to solve. Hundreds of tons of sand had to be removed to expose the strewn portions of flattened and twisted wreckage. The pods would not permit the divers to work. They would block the air-lift nozzle, roll into any crater made in the sand with the air-lift and fill it in minutes with a mass of brown decaying red bait.

We tried using our water blower together with the lift hose, one diver blowing the pods away and holding them at bay while the second diver vacuumed the sand layer away. The pods always returned to fill the cleared area. Like an army of ETs, they floated in the sea, returning to their positions again and again, brown monsters bobbing and descending to engulf the toiling divers.

Paul van der Merwe designed and built a little gadget to inject air into them. He was going to take on the 'cucumbers', as they became known, one by one, inflate them with air and float them up to the surface to burst or be carried away by the currents. It did not work. His device blew apart with the first attempt.

As the pods always returned and drifted into any hole we made, we decided to give them one. Sucking a wide deep hole off the site, the divers watched in glee as the advance of the mindless pods began. Hundreds and hundreds drifted into the hole, piling themselves into the crater. Using the blower we blew the pods in the working area towards the hole. In they went filling the metres-deep cavity. Then we covered them with a layer of sand directed there by the blower. Buried, they stayed there and that was that.

Galley stove top plate

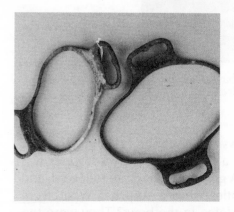

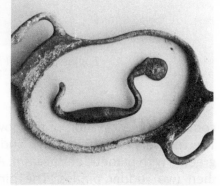

Pot-holders for carrying hot pots aboard ship   *Pot-holder*

Only eight artefacts were found during the first month of work. Spirits plunged. To endure weeks of toil, hours of intensive planning and daily mooring of the *Reunion* with virtually no results was most disheartening. Empty sand down to bedrock greeted each pair of weary divers time and time again. The top plate of a galley stove emerged, then a bin hinge, then nothing. We were determined to

Fire-hose couplings

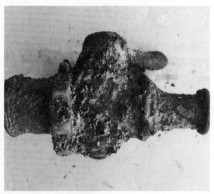

Fire-hose nozzle and valve

Engine gear-shift base plate

complete the excavation of the bows and continued cleaning the site. The recovery of a brass valve and a pipe fitting with a stopper was greeted with pathetic enthusiasm. A gearshift base plate followed, and then two rudder pintles. The pintles were a surprise. What were pintles, the supports for a rudder, doing in the bows? They were too large to have been part of a lifeboat, each requiring a strong man to lift them. They could only have belonged to the rudder of the *Birkenhead* herself. We examined them closely. They were new pintles: there was no sign of any marking or scoring on their pins to indicate that they had been in use. We concluded they were spare pintles, large brass pivots used to couple the rudder to the stern, still intact after all those years.

We were joined on the *Reunion* by Albert Botha as extra diver. He was tall, powerfully built and immensely strong, and one simply had to

Button of the 74th Regiment with crown and elephant, commemorating the Battle of Assaye

Regimental buttons

Badges of 6th and 91st Regiments and square Gibraltar badge of the Royal Marines after cleaning

Stamped square brass badge of the Royal Marines with lion and crown. On the left, the face has been worn by the sea. On the right, a painted plaster of Paris mould made from the intact back of the worn badge – Gibraltar, per mare per terram

Pewter regimental buttons on the left and brass shirt buttons on the right

Close-up of Allport pistol's silver label

look at a heavy motor or piece of equipment that needed moving and he would effortlessly lift it and place it in its new position.

Work on the bows moved back to the O to S, 10 to 14 section of the grid. This corresponded to the portion of the bows that had accompanied the engine during the second break of the vessel, the part immediately in front of the engine-room and extending forward to the foremast.

We needed to know what we could expect to find. Each artefact would give us information about where we were on the vessel. Looking at the plans, we decided that on the upper deck we might find rigging, cap pegs, muskets, hammocks and knapsacks with their contents. The main deck held the chief engineer's cabin, his wash-house and mess, and the troop mess. Below, on the lower deck, was the engineer's storeroom and another mess. The hold held chain lockers, ballast tanks, the shell room, magazine and light room. The light room was immediately forward of the magazine. Light in the dark confines of the hold was provided by oil-burning gimbal-mounted lamps. Entering a magazine containing gunpowder with a flame was avoided by using the light room where lamps could be lit in safety and their light then used to see in the magazine.

We located copper pot lids, a brass oil funnel, a double wooden pulley, a deck skylight and lens, and a shaving brush cup – all mute testimony to life on the *Birkenhead*. Towards the end of March a brass bell crown piece was found. At first it was not recognised for what it was, as it was simply a broken piece of metal with four curved arms, one of which was missing. Mike Keulemans noticed that the broken surface had a ground glinting appearance. He had worked on the conservation of several maritime bells and noticed the resemblance. With his guidance and explanation, the picture emerged. It was the support eye for a bell, the claw used to hang the bell.

The implication was unpleasant, for it meant that the bell of the *Birkenhead* was destroyed and gone forever. Tromp van Diggelen's dream of returning the *Birkenhead* bell to England was over. To prove that it was indeed a bell, I sent a small piece of the broken arm for analysis. This showed a composition of tin (18,3%), lead (4,8%), iron (0,12%), aluminium (less than 0,1%), zinc (0%) and copper (76,68%). Discussion with a metallurgist revealed that this was bell metal used up to the 1890s. Lead was added to facilitate machining and improve tone. Modern bells use 20–25% tin and the rest copper. No further trace of the bell could be found.

A small medicine bottle, intact and sealed with a ground-glass stopper, was found in the same area (S11) as the shaving cup, as well as gold-plated buttons with tiny, marvellously detailed facsimiles of the Forester engines of the *Birkenhead* set in bas-relief. The area corresponded to Chief Engineer Whyham's cabin.

Right in the middle of the Q12 grid was Grant's condenser, the 'treasure chest' that Pierre and I had chanced upon during the earlier dives. It was a landmark for most divers visiting the *Birkenhead*. Plating had to be removed nearby and, fearing that the condenser might be damaged by a moving plate, we strapped and lifted it from the sand. The whole team watched in fascination as the *Reunion*'s winch slowly brought the condenser to the surface. A greenish gold haze appeared in the water, which gradually assumed a rectangular shape. Then willing hands guided the condenser as it slid over the sloping back of the deck and was pulled to rest in front of the winch. Using the fire-hose, we pumped fresh sea water through its piping. Sand, worms, cone shells, a little octopus, a minute crab, and baby crayfish just a few millimetres in length came flushing out. Grant's condenser had been a safe home for thousands of tiny creatures. As all the sand disappeared, the whole complex array of cooling pipes and steam inlet and exhaust became clear. It was in very good condition.

We were searching for the magazine at the time. It had been a large area nearly 7 m in length and supposedly had several hundred double-barrelled rifles of a new design destined for the 9th Lancers. We were finding remarkably few artefacts despite the fact that divers were working all day, every day, on site, except in rough seas. A few musket balls and a gunpowder keg stave boosted our interest but that was all. The entire magazine and its contents eluded us. I discussed this with Captain Okkie Grapow one evening at his home. The specific gravity of gunpowder is almost exactly one and when contained in a wooden barrel held together with fibrous netting (metal hoops posed a spark hazard) the barrel would float. Possibly all the gunpowder simply floated away following the breakup and sinking. But where were all the rifles, shot for the cannons, musket balls for the troops, and light room lamps? We had found the stern but the forward magazine had disappeared.

Two months had elapsed, 21 artefacts had been located, and the work continued. A copper pot lid, a copper stove cover plate, a jelly mould, and a brass porthole frame were found in the galley S8 area. P12 yielded a wine bottle base with the moulded words 'Ricketts Bristol', confirming Mr Molyneux-Berry's assessment of the previous year. It also contained another porthole frame, a cold cream jar lid and broken plate shards. The Q12-14 grid held conglomerated musket balls, two hairbrushes, a bottle with the words 'Lea and Perrins', the

Bronze pulleys

headpiece of a drum major's mace, brass pulleys and brackets, buckles and an oil-drip cup. Each section provided a few portions of the vessel's piping and pulleys, remnants of her lamps, traces of the troops' equipment, and isolated personal items. There was as yet nothing coherent, only a few pieces here and there buried in sand, scattered by the fall of the bows down the rock and the sea currents. After almost three months of work the divers had moved back from the bows, past the empty and barren sand between the paddles towards the boilers. Beyond the boilers, the hard, dense, black conglomerated stern once more awaited us.

With the regular strenuous diving, the spectre of the bends appeared. We were using the United States Navy surface decompression diving tables. Charlie experienced shoulder pain after some of his dives, and Mike developed 'sparkles' in his vision and tingling in his foot. Paul developed an elbow pain and Malcolm vague aches. Rambo emerged from the decompression chamber with a ferocious itch on his chest and back and a flaring red rash over these areas. He was getting 'skin bends'. In each case, the diver had to be put back into the chamber for a prolonged period of therapeutic decompression on oxygen.

Something had to be done to stop these bends. If we had a few days of bad weather, which put a halt to diving, our subsequent diving was bends-free for a while, but inevitably pains or itch returned. We increased the time spent in the chamber after each dive, but this made very little difference. I decided to try and find the fault in the tables we were using. They were obviously inadequate for our hard and regular diving regime.

A series of curves was drawn, representing the uptake of nitrogen in different tissues. Serious errors in our diving routine became apparent. The divers were ascending too fast, even though they were following recommended rates, and the initial depth at which the chamber was set was too shallow. The tables were modified and the bends disappeared. There was a bonus in store. The curves also indicated that the modified tables would enable a diver to perform a second dive each day. This was tested and proved. From then on the divers who worked the first few 80-minute shifts of the day spent a further 60 minutes at the site later that afternoon. This meant that two or three pairs of divers could each spend a total of 140 minutes a day at a depth of 30 m. Our efficiency under water soared!

Tabulating the curves gave us a list of schedules for dives from 20 m to 60 m with air as the breathing medium. Later that year I was very gratified to hear that the tables had been successfully used on work on the *Borderer*, a wreck at a depth of nearly 50 m near Struisbaai.

After surfacing the divers spent 40 minutes in the decompression chamber, lying down and breathing pure oxygen all the time. They were invariably tired after their stint under water and, eyes closed and half asleep, they rested until their time under pressure was up. When they transferred to the entrance lock, the pressure was reduced to surface pressure over five minutes. There was a steady roar of vented air and a thick cloudy fog formed in the lock. Joining the men on the deck, they would discuss their dive and the progress of the work.

Shirts off and enjoying the sun, they watched flocks of cormorants and gannets wheeling and diving into the sea as they followed the shoals of sardines around the coast.

We had other visitors as well. Seals, curious and intrigued by our daily arrival, came to call. Sometimes they came alone, but more often two or more turned up. With their big brown long-lashed eyes looking at us over their whiskered snouts they resembled mournful clowns. Sometimes they would simply sunbathe on the surface, lifting a fore-flipper and enjoying the warmth on their bodies. On other occasions, they would buzz the divers at the *Birkenhead*, startling them with a high-speed mock attack. Brushing past in a swooping curve, the seal would stop and turn, sharp teeth exposed in a grin of pure mischief.

There was a large resident red roman at the *Birkenhead*. Curious too, he regularly came right up to the working diver to see what he was doing. Sometimes it took a clip on the nose to remind him not to interfere in our business. He became a sort of pet, and although we often had a good fish meal from the area, the red roman was taboo.

When I first saw the *Birkenhead* I was amazed that coral flourished on the wreck. I had always believed coral required warm tropical waters, and had expected the wreck to be bleak and stark. Not so! To the unaided eye, everything appears brown and green because the water filters out all other colours at a depth of 30 m. A waterproof light creates a fairyland. Bright pinks, oranges, reds, purples and yellows appear. The wreck and the surrounding rocks come alive with brightly coloured corals and sponges.

Sharks were a factor when we first planned our diving techniques. We decided firmly against in-water decompressions. The large fish factory at Gansbaai has the jaws of several huge sharks prominently displayed above the front door of the fish shop. We saw fishermen bringing home netted sharks by the dozen, laying them on the jetty in the harbour with their savagely toothed mouths half open and their dead eyes staring at the sky. In January 1987, the largest great white shark ever netted in South African waters was caught at Gansbaai. It was 6 m long and weighed a massive 1 241 kg!

Near Birkenhead Rock is Dyer Island, the breeding ground of thousands of seals, and the home of our sad-eyed visitors. Each year, the pups fall easy prey to the great white sharks that prowl the waters. Perhaps the hubbub of our expedition discouraged them, or perhaps sharks no longer visit the *Birkenhead* area. Perhaps we were just plain lucky. The sharks left us alone and we never complained.

The use of the *Reunion* and the experience the divers had gained permitted them to work in far rougher seas than they would have attempted while on the *Adventurer*. Working at the decompression chamber one day, I noticed a change in the movement of the *Reunion* and, looking up, saw that we had changed our mooring position. The wave, previously to our port side, was now to starboard! Surprised, I gazed up at the bridge. There was Ernie, bellowing orders and yelling for immediate action. One of our mooring ropes had parted and, quietly and quickly, the current had swung the *Reunion* around the rock. Had divers been below, their hoses would have dragged them across the wall of the pinnacle. Had the direction of the current been a little more southerly, the vessel would have hit the peak. We were reminded that our presence was accepted only on sufferance.

A rope parted on another occasion as well. The weather was rapidly worsening, the divers had been recalled, and we were making ready to lift the water blower from the bottom. A massive wave sent a plough of water hammering against the *Reunion*, breaking right over the chamber, the deck and the men. The port stern mooring snapped. The two hydraulic steel-reinforced hoses to the blower suddenly began stretching as the blower dragged along the bottom and jammed against a rock. Fearful of snaring the hoses in his propellers, Ernie could not start his engines. Charlie ran aft, knife in hand, ready to cut the hoses. The blower pulled free, the hosing slackened and hands flashed as the blower was hauled aboard in record time!

In April sovereigns were again located on the port side of the stern. Excitement heralded the find of eight George IV and nine Victoria gold coins. The hope, the plea, in each man's mind was that at last we had located the legendary pay packet. Within three days another 28 sovereigns emerged, together with three Victoria half-sovereigns and two Victoria half-crowns. Feelings were mixed. If we had located the area where the 120 boxes of gold and silver coins had been stored, why were we finding coins in small numbers? We should be uncovering sovereigns in their thousands. Were we at the periphery of a scatter of coins, with the bulk enclosed within the central mass of the conglomerated stern? The following week brought twelve sovereigns and 24 April another nineteen. By the end of the season a total of 111 coins was in safe deposit and in bond, including those found the previous year.

As the divers slowly progressed into the conglomerate, they reached the ship's surgery, where a silver trocar and cannula, a silver catheter, and a sealed glass bottle, still full of mercury, were found. These surely belonged to Dr Culhane, the ship's surgeon. I have often quietly speculated on the connection between the catheter and the mercury. In those days the cause of syphilis was unknown, but mercury was certainly used in its treatment. A ship full of young men, a foreign destination – who knows?

A magnificent brass telescope labelled 'Wm. Ashmore. Achromatic London', still intact and functional, was added to over 30 artefacts recovered during the last three days of diving. These included the inclinometer of the *Birkenhead* (a device that measured the angle as she rolled in the sea), a jar lid, a silver fork, a brass rifle butt plate, a musket ball mould, skylight prisms, brass handles, hinges and posts, and then, just before the season closed, two nameplates.

One was found in the H3 area and bore the inscription 'R.S. Bond'. This was Ralph Sheldon-Bond, the cornet of the 12th Lancers who

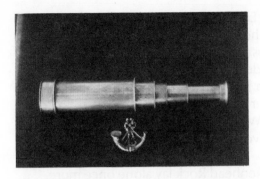

Brass telescope with badge of the 43rd Regiment

survived the disaster, found his horse on the beach and 'had great luck in saving 150 sovereigns'.

The other came from the F3 site. It stated simply 'Alexander Seton'. Lieutenant-Colonel Alexander Seton of the 74th Highlanders, the officer commanding all the troops, the man who had ordered the soldiers to stand fast on deck to save the women and children, and who died as the *Birkenhead* died.

Names from the past, cherished and remembered by their regiments, returned from the sea to await their place of pride.

The weather was turning once more, the wind coming more and more often from the north-west with rain, high seas, and storms. Sometimes, on reaching the site, we found that diving conditions were too dangerous and returned to Gansbaai harbour. These aborted trips became known as 'the breakfast run', as the only useful thing accomplished was a meal. On other occasions a dive would be started, only to be called off when it became obvious that we were looking for trouble. Once, after such an aborted dive, the *Reunion* had rounded Danger Point on her way home. A large swell was running from behind and the vessel was making record time. Rambo's wife was aboard, sitting on the starboard stern rail enjoying the wind and the speed. Suddenly, a giant swell appeared astern and rapidly bore down on the *Reunion*. Her stern lifted high in the huge swell and she broached, turning sideways into the water. The bows ploughed down into the sea and she rolled over to starboard. One funnel, our large air compressor, our hot-water machine and a terrified Mrs Rambo disappeared under water.

The men on the bridge and in the galley were hurled against the wall as the *Reunion* rolled through 90 degrees. The divers decompressing in the chamber banged against its steel sides and stared unbelievingly at the sea through the round window in the roof. Visions of being trapped under pressure in a steel container on a sinking ship flashed through their minds!

Hanging on to his controls, Ernie turned hard to starboard, forcing the ship into the direction of the wave. Like a corkscrew the *Reunion* responded. Her plunging bows surfaced, her stern swung round and, streaming sea water from her decks, she righted herself. On the stern rail, arms and legs clinging in a leech-like embrace, the half-drowned Mrs Rambo emerged. She never did accompany us again.

The work for 1987 was over. We did not wish to repeat the loss of the moorings, so the *Causeway Salvor* arrived again to winch the buoys on board.

As the *Salvor* left the site, Birkenhead Rock lay alone once more.

Key-tag: Captain Lockers

Key-tag: Steerage Port no. 6. Note the broad arrow

Ensign G.A. Lucas's nameplate. He later became Chief Magistrate of Natal and initiated the first 'Birkenhead Syndicate' to search for the gold

Nameplate of Ralph Sheldon-Bond, Cornet of the 12th Lancers, who was in charge of the horses

Wine bottle

Small medicine bottle

Nameplate of Lieutenant-Colonel Alexander Seton of the 74th Highlanders, the officer in overall charge of the troops, who ordered the men to stand fast on the sinking poop deck

A bottle containing mercury

BELOW LEFT: *Glass bottle*
BELOW RIGHT: *Lea and Perrins bottle with chilis*

Reconstructing the Disaster

After two summers at the site of the wreck, a great deal had been learned about the distribution of the remnants of the *Birkenhead*. The position of the fairleads, the large openings high on the bows through which the bow anchor chains passed, had been mapped. Chain still ran from the fairleads, lying broken on the sandy sea floor, to the bow anchor higher up on the rock, indicating that the *Birkenhead* had still been anchored to the rock when she began to break up.

On a ledge at the base of the rock rested the large forward capstan and, south-west of this, the huge engines lay on their sides, still almost intact. Originally these had been directly between the paddles. Now they were 20 m forward. How had the engines come to land so far forward? Their sheared crankshafts showed where they had ripped free of the paddle shafts, and large torn pipes told of their fractured boiler couplings. Straddling an empty expanse of sand where the engines should have been, the two large paddle shafts with their hubs lay in almost perfect original alignment just in front of the boilers.

The process of the breakup of the *Birkenhead* was there for us to read. We had spent months and months on careful research above and below water. We had collated evidence and facts. We had argued and discussed, and we could now give a much fuller account of how she sank that fateful night so many years ago.

Her bows rammed the pinnacle which ripped open the plates to flood the forward area. The paddles continued to tear up the water, setting up a fierce vibration that weakened the engine mountings, the boiler couplings and the crankshafts connecting the engines to the paddles. Thrusting and pushing, the *Birkenhead* attempted to climb up and over the peak, shudderingly impaling herself harder on to the rock. Her hull rivets made only of iron (steel had not yet been invented) were never intended for this type of strain and moment by moment the hull weakened. The engines were stopped, giving pause to the savage hammering the ship was taking. The bow anchor was dropped to prevent the vessel from falling back into deeper water until the damage could be assessed. Rattling through the fairlead, the bow anchor hooked on to the rock.

The *Birkenhead* was grinding heavily in the swell on the rock. A turn astern was commanded to free the *Birkenhead* from the peak. Her two-pistoned 350 horsepower Forester engines thumped into activity again. At the top of each piston a long arm moved the centrally pivoted and massive engine beam which in turn was coupled to the two heavy paddle crankshafts 8 m above the bottom deck. Vibrating fiercely, the *Birkenhead* shifted. As she moved back, the bow anchor chain pulled tight, forcing the bows, filled with water and much less buoyant, to drop and smash the bowsprit and the figurehead of Vulcan. The plates of the engine-room ground on the ledge below the rocky crest, tearing open a huge gash in the bilge hull. Tons of water gushed into the engine-room. The juddering engine was flooded and the boiler fires were extinguished. Hot steam pipes, suddenly cooled by the cold sea and shaken violently by the engine movement, fractured.

Drifting just off the rock but held to it by the bow anchor, the *Birkenhead* wallowed heavily, her central area flooded and held afloat only by her holed forward area and the still buoyant stern.

About fifteen minutes had passed since the impact. Still chained to the rock, the bows tore off just behind the foremast as weakened rivets and plating ripped. Tumbling down the rock, the bows crashed into the sand on the seabed, trailing debris and streaming chain through the fairlead to the anchor higher up on the pinnacle. The forward capstan broke free and came to rest on a narrow shelf near the base of the rock. The weight of the engines and boilers sent the flooded middle section deeper into the sea, canting the stern and its assembled troops up into the air. Again the *Birkenhead* tore, this time from the front of the engine-room down and astern, below the paddles and to the front of the boilers. Every single attachment between the engine and the boilers was severed. At the same time, the crankshafts coupling the paddles to the engines sheared, leaving the two paddle wheels and their shafts completely free and suspended high up in the ship. Instantly sinking, the engines and what was left of the bows tumbled and rolled down the rock to its base, nearly 30 m below the surface.

Half of the ship – from the boilers to the rudder – remained. Water poured in through the opened boiler section and gushed through open bulkheads to swamp the entire stern. Relieved of the weight of the engines, the stern fell back from its steep tilt and on an even keel it rapidly settled in the water and disappeared. It came to rest almost exactly on a north-south line on the sandy bottom of a gully at the base of the rock.

To this day the orientation of the various sections remains – from the bow anchor, chain and fairleads to the lie of the paddle wheels with the empty space where the engines were, to the shattered boiler, and then back to the crumpled tiller arm on the stern.

The Third Expedition

The coming season would be our third year at the site and, at its end, the divers would have spent one year of their lives swimming at the wreck or moored above it.

Very little had changed when I reached the harbour in January 1988. The smell of the factory, the fishing boats, the quay – all were just the same. The *Reunion* was at her berth and our equipment was on board and fully functional. South African Diving Services once again lent us a chamber, which was firmly welded to the port-side deck. To balance its weight, our shining two-ton air-lift compressor was fixed to the star-board side.

We had bought the compressor the previous year to power sand removal at the site of the wreck. Italo had seen it standing in the front garden of an old house in Benoni. Arriving at my home he said, 'Come, I want to show you something.' While driving to Benoni he described the machine in glowing terms, how it was just what we needed, and how powerful it was. I gazed at the dented and rusted cover of the faded blue derelict with horror.

'How much do they want for this thing?' I asked.

'Only 3 600 rands,' he replied happily.

'Oh!' I said. 'Are you sure its alright?'

That was a stupid question to ask Italo. He promptly opened the cover and began checking the compressor, crawling under it quite oblivious of the fact that he was getting filthy. He emerged streaked with grease. 'Yes,' he said.

'But does it start?' I asked, still doubtful.

Another stupid question. He turned the ignition key and the machine wheezed. 'Not really,' he replied, 'she's got an inter-stage pressure build-up. This causes excess loading and blockage on her first stage and this stalls her.'

'Oh!' I said, concentrating on a large spider web on the battery. I did not have the faintest idea what he was talking about.

'But it's nothing much, I'll just fix her,' he continued, looking fondly at the constipated ruin.

He did. In one day the compressor was roaring and venting air by the megalitre. Two days later she was gleaming and bright yellow.

Diving at the *Birkenhead* recommenced on 19 January 1988. The area immediately behind the boilers contained engine spares. Very prominent was the spare engine beam lying half-buried in sand on hull plate on the starboard side of the wreck. Next to it and straddling the long axis of the stern was a spare engine shaft for coupling the beam to the paddles. The engine beam was 7 m long and the shaft 5 m long. Both were very heavy.

The *Birkenhead* could expect no assistance with spares on her voyages and had to carry her own. Brass valves, bronze bearings, hinges and base plates were found. The area corresponded to the I to K, 6 to 8 grid and extended into the store area found during 1986. A copper tag in the port I7 square orientated us. It stated 'Steerage Port No. 6'. The same square yielded two leather pouches, a leather belt, a brush, an eight-ounce earthenware pot (in two pieces), a wooden mallet head and a brass label engraved 'Brown Brothers'.

An interesting aspect of the salvage was the deductive work involved. We had already had some experience with Mr Whyham's buttons and medicine, Dr Culhane's catheter and mercury, gunner John Archbold's calipers, and the spare rudder pintles in the bow. This was to continue. A brass badge bearing the number 91 was found in the G7 area and, later, a brass clip of the type used to suspend medals. Not much in itself, but the implications were fascinating. A brass badge in the stern indicated an officer's badge. There was only one officer of the 91st Regiment on board, Captain Edward Wright.

Finding a copper key tag with the words 'Purser's Steward' in the same area provided a second clue; it had to do with the layout of the cabins.

All the women and children were quartered in the back of the stern on both sides of the lower deck, their cabins opening on to a central passage which led forward to the stern mess. Right in front of the ladies' accommodation were two other cabins, one on either side of the passage. Facing forward, the purser's steward's cabin was to the left and an officer's cabin to the right. This was the only officer's cabin on the lower deck, all the others being one flight up on the main deck. Both cabins opened only into the mess. There was no access to the passage leading to the ladies' quarters. These were, after all, Victorian times!

It would appear that Captain Wright was the only officer to share the deck with the ladies. It is also interesting that he above all others exhorted the troops to maintain their positions on the doomed vessel

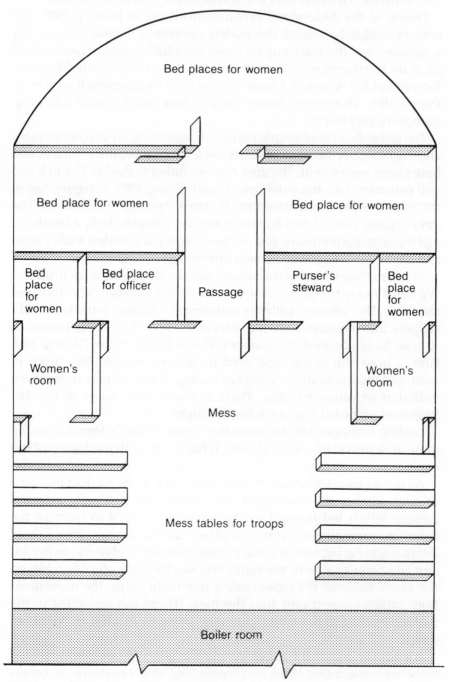

Bed places for women

Bed place for women

Bed place for women

Bed place for women

Bed place for officer

Passage

Purser's steward

Bed place for women

Women's room

Women's room

Mess

Mess tables for troops

Boiler room

Diagram of bed places on lower deck

and allow the women and children to be saved. An empty wine bottle completed the findings in his quarters.

More and more artefacts emerged as the days passed. They were fascinating, emerging from a broken sandwich of the four decks of the *Birkenhead*. Remnants of each tier were found, but not in any order. Upper deck wooden pulleys, sheaves, and a lifeboat rowlock were interspersed with main deck remnants, such as brass doorknobs, locking plates, and portions of oil lamps and portholes. Military items, comprising pistols, rifles, sword handles, brass belt buckles and clips, musket balls, signal gun shot, and a grapeshot canister end with shot accompanied more personal items, such as a cast ornamental piece, silver teaspoons, silver forks, crystal glass fragments, a silver-plated letter opener, an earthenware ink-well, hairbrushes, shaving brushes, a gold-plated decoration with the words '... oit Peninsula', a hip flask and bottles – hundreds of artefacts, each with a story to tell.

A wind-in brass tape measure calibrated in inches and still functional was found in J8 directly behind the boiler room on the starboard side. I was not surprised to see whose cabin this had been. Immediately

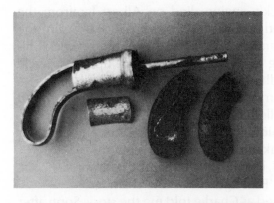

Portions of Allport pistol

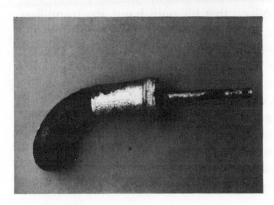

Henry Allport pepper box pistol

forward of gunner John Archbold's cabin, it belonged to J. Roberts, the ship's carpenter. Other remnants of his room were a brass oil lamp base, a wooden pulley block, a wooden mallet head, a brass door-keep and lock plate, and two lead plates labelled six and five pounds. We also found leather shoe pieces and a sock. Roberts died when the *Birkenhead* sank.

We used the 'rubber duck', a little inflatable boat with a small petrol engine, to haul the mooring lines to the buoys each day. This was a duty much disliked because it was invariably cold and the sea choppy. Divers, while perfectly happy under water, hate to be wet with their clothing on. The south-east buoy was especially abhorred. It was very close to the rock and right in the action of the wave. The rubber duck would approach warily, one man holding the mooring line in his hand while lying stretched out in the front of the boat, ready to shackle the rope to the loop on the buoy. Another man guided the boat, primed for a speedy getaway should the wave appear.

At the end of each day the ropes had to be unshackled and manually hauled aboard.

One day the rubber duck's engine died on Albert far from the moored *Reunion*. He pulled the starting cord again and again, the heavy muscles on his arms and back quivering with the power of his effort. Eventually the starting mechanism simply gave up the struggle and came apart. There was Albert, alone and stranded in his boat.

Nick grabbed a rope, swam to the rubber duck and remained with Albert while the boat was pulled aboard.

That night I awoke near midnight. Italo hit me hard on the shoulder and bellowed, 'Hey Allan, wake up!'

'What's going on?' I yelled, irritated by his method of arousal.

'Albert's bent,' he replied. 'Paul's got him in the chamber.'

Dressing hurriedly, I listened as Charlie told me the story. Soon after arriving home, Albert had noticed that his right hand was trembling. Not wanting to create a fuss, he had ignored it. Later that night the tremor became a rapid unco-ordinated twitching. The others became alarmed when they saw the totally abstinent Albert jerkily slopping liquid from a glass.

We drove to the *Reunion* where Paul was watching over Albert in the chamber, pressurised to a water depth of 18 m and breathing pure oxygen via a face mask. He had already improved and the tremor had gone. A bend like this meant that his nervous system had been affected. Bubbles of nitrogen had formed in his brain or upper spinal cord. One had to regard this as much more sinister than a skin itch or shoulder ache, and the four hours and forty-five minute Table 6 therapeutic decompression schedule of the U.S. Navy was needed. A long night lay ahead and André kept me company as the others went home. They had to be ready to dive again in the morning.

Albert had bent because of the intense exertion in trying to start the motor. Nitrogen in solution in his tissues and harmlessly degassing had bubbled free with the exercise. The bubbles had interfered with the blood supply to that portion of his nervous system controlling co-ordination of his right hand, hence the tremor.

In addition to his big appetite, Albert has another singular characteristic. He sleeps a lot. Between dives, after meals or during any quiet period he would lie down on a bunk, a coiled rope, or the deck and sleep.

That night we needed him awake: it was essential that he breathed the oxygen properly to redissolve the bubbles and flush the nitrogen from his tissues. Should he fall asleep, his breathing would become too shallow and slow. This was a herculean task. We made him drink water until he threatened to hit us, we shone lights in his eyes, we banged on the chamber walls, and we made him read. At nearly 04h00 he emerged symptom-free and, exhausted, we all went home.

The divers were making an impression on the conglomerate at last. For two years it had defied all attempts to investigate its contents. Removing the surrounding sand and clearing under the conglomerate provided a solution. Tunnelling under the wreck from both sides created a network of channels through which slings could be passed. These were connected to the *Reunion*'s winch and the sea did the rest. The upward and downward movement of the vessel in the swells alternately tugged on the conglomerate and released the pressure. One just had to be patient. The slow repetitive pulls gradually caused cracking. When slack occurred in the cable it was gently taken up.

As penetration progressed, plates were lifted and cleared. Some days were spent solely on cleaning up and removing rocks and debris. It was much easier to explore a properly exposed area than grope under rocks and decayed iron.

Work concentrated on the starboard side of the wreck and artefacts from the starboard officers' cabins, the lower deck mess, and the spirit room in the hold were found. These included shaving brushes, a little brass bell, bottles, bits of porcelain and pottery, military remnants and sovereigns.

In all, 44 sovereigns were found, mostly damaged Victoria coins. There were also two George IV, one George III and one William IV sovereigns and ten pennies and six half-pennies. No one had any doubt at this stage that we were finding personal monies. We knew we were in the officers' quarters and could expect them to have had money with them. Our total sovereign count was now 155.

On 12 March 1988 a meeting took place in Gansbaai. Present were two representatives of the British Embassy, Advocate B. Hofmann of the Department of Foreign Affairs, Mr A. Schmidt of the Department of Customs and Excise, Jalmar Rudner from the National Monuments Council, Okkie Grapow from Pentow Marine, and ourselves. They had come to see what we were doing and what we had achieved.

Italo's *Splash Dance* was ready at the harbour to take the party to the *Reunion*, already on site and working. It was cold and overcast and the sea calm. Italo, never one to stand on ceremony, used his usual boating technique. He opened the throttles wide and we roared to sea. Our guests smiled bravely while they clutched the railings as they bounced on the hard deck of *Splash Dance*. As we passed Danger Point and reached the swells of the open ocean, the thumping increased and the wind ballooned clothing out, matching frozen bodies to already numbed minds.

We circled the *Reunion* and the site, watching the men on the deck and the hoses to the divers disappearing down into the grey sea. There was no wave that day and the rock remained sullenly submerged. Because there was very little gratification in watching bubbles surfacing from working men, we returned to shore to see the artefacts, plans, maps, coins and photographs, and have a hot cup of coffee at Die Kelders.

The discussion was confined to the wrecking and the artefacts. The sensitive question of British interest in the *Birkenhead* and the war grave issue were studiously avoided. But, for the first time, we had the opportunity to demonstrate to all what we were doing and openly discuss our progress. Within a few months the conflict regarding ownership was to be finally resolved.

The stern area had been explored thoroughly, and there was no longer any place where thousands of coins could remain hidden. The stern did not contain the pay packet.

Attention once again focussed on the elusive magazine. The engines had been directly behind the forward magazine and the two had broken off as a single piece. Could the magazine be under the engines, deeply buried in sand?

The divers concentrated their efforts at the base of the rock where the two large engines lay on their sides, one on top of the other. Soon after sand removal commenced Nick found a sovereign! We no longer had any choice. The area under the massive engines had to be examined.

Lifting them was another matter. Each piston was over 3 m in diameter. The heavy supports and beams were triple that in length. We had no desire to salvage them at that stage as we lacked the facilities to restore such large objects, and allowing them to decay on the surface was unthinkable. They could, however, be moved to one side, allowing access to the sand beneath them.

The heavy-duty winch cable of the *Reunion* was fixed to the top engine. Italo watched at the bottom as the engine trembled with the force of the pull. It refused to budge.

When he reached the surface he was greeted by the incredible sight of the *Reunion* standing up on her stern, canted over to port by the cable's pull and her bows rearing clear of the sea! She had the heart but not the power to lift the engines.

The divers began to excavate under the engines. In some places the bed was rocky and in others the sand shelved deeply. Clearing was dangerous, as the engines could shift with the undermining of their support and crush a diver. It took two days to be sure. The magazine was not under the engines, nor were the boxes of specie.

Since work had been redirected to the bows, attention moved to the area above the engines and up the face of the rock. Just above the ledge where the forward capstan had come to rest, was a sand-filled gully cutting into the pinnacle. Whale-shaped, it was about 15 m long and 4 m wide at the front, tapering backwards to a point. Near the 'tail' in grid area X12 we made one of the most important finds of the expedition.

The *Birkenhead* hold had included a store-room in the bows, one deck below the troop mess and immediately behind the gunner's store-room, the most forward room on the lowest deck. When the first break in the ship occurred, the bows had crashed down the rock, spraying contents from its stores which cascaded to the rocky base. The gully had acted as a trap, collecting then covering scattered items with a layer of sand.

On clearing away the sand, we found artefacts in their thousands. Bone brush handles, their bristles mostly gone, appeared. Most had four-digit numbers on them. Many also had regimental numbers and names inscribed.

As examples, artefact no. 493 had 74th.F. 3125 E.Mc L.; no. 497, 74th. D3195 A.B.; and 516, 91st. 27 .. J. Holden. Referring to the name list revealed that these were privates Edward MacLeod and Archbold Baxter of the 74th Highlanders, and John Holden of the 91st Regiment.

The last was the only survivor of the three.

Bone shaving brushes, silver spoons, bone knife handles and cut-throat razor handles were then found, again inscribed with regiment, number and name.

Over the next few days nearly a thousand regimental buttons emerged, together with 600 webbing buckles, tassel holders, brass plate buckles and badges of the 6th, 12th, 73rd and 91st Regiment. Near the front of the gully an earthenware jar packed with percussion caps was a splendid find.

Cleaned badges of the
73rd and
12th Regiment

After five days the gully was cleared and work once more moved back to the stern. Back-to-back with the boiler room and a little to port on the main deck was Dr Culhane's dispensary. It corresponded to the area K6 on our plan and in it we found five medicine bottles, a square bottle, a medicine measure and a pocket watch, the latter probably belonging to the horse-riding doctor himself.

Only two days remained. Once again winter was approaching and the salvage had to close. On 24 April 1988 the *Reunion* travelled to Birkenhead Rock for the very last time. The last of the artefacts were gathered and stored, and the salvage of HMS *Birkenhead* paused.

Some of the questions posed by the sinking of HMS *Birkenhead* have been solved. We proved that the stern had not gone missing. We also learned a great deal about the breakup of the ship. The legendary gold eluded us, as it had escaped all others before us. We had reasoned that it was loaded in the stern. This could not have been so. Even if previous salvors had found the pay packet, it is extremely unlikely that they would have been able to remove every single box. Some scatter or entrapment must have occurred and we would have found evidence of it.

Tromp van Diggelen wrote in his prospectus that divers had been sent to the wreck on three occasions by the Navy over a period of 80 years. Training exercises or salvage? We had spent three summers on the wreck, battling with sand, rocks, conglomerate, plating, red bait and iron beams. Up-to-date technology and diving techniques had enabled us to spend more time at the wreck site than any other salvage in history. With our first-hand knowledge of the difficulties involved, we consider it inconceivable for over three tons of coinage to have been completely removed in a brief period or a few short dives.

The forward magazine also eluded us. At the time of the wreck, gunpowder and arms were in very short supply in the Cape Colony. Charlie and I spent a day at the archives of the South African Library in Cape Town, perusing the official documents and letters that passed between the British government and the governor at the Cape, Sir Harry Smith. We learnt that there had been an active trafficking in stolen arms and powder and that anyone caught in this activity was summarily executed without the formality of a trial. The magazine of the troopship Birkenhead would have been laden with extra munitions for the frontier war.

The location of a packed magazine and massive engines was precisely where the vessel hit the submerged ledge on her second strike. She was holed in the heaviest part of her structure. Her bulkheads had been penetrated and modified with hatches for easy troop transfer. Add to this an iron hull and rivets, a fiercely vibrating engine and side-paddles grinding her against a pinnacle, and the reasons for her rapid breakup become clearer.

With the constant shifting and movement of the sand, the heavy magazine will have settled down to bed-rock. Somewhere near the base of Birkenhead Rock, deeply buried under sand, the magazine lies. The magazine of a troopship was always guarded. Was it in the magazine that the specie was stored?

In June 1988 I heard the news. Accord between the British and South African governments had been reached. As both sides had interest in the wreck, a compromise had been found. The portion of the artefacts claimed by the National Monuments Council would be shared between the two countries and distributed among museums designated by them. Should the pay packet be discovered, this would be shared in the same fashion as the artefacts.

On 8 October 1988 the official division of the artefacts took place at the Cultural History Museum in Cape Town. Representing the museum was Dr Bruno Werz, the newly appointed marine archaeologist, and Mr Anton Roux, director of the museum. Also present was a representative of the British Embassy. Following the division, our share of artefacts was retained by the museum for study and photography. Early in January 1989 our portion was returned to us, and definitive restoration was commenced.

Epilogue

A plaque on the lighthouse at Danger Point commemorates the sinking of HMS *Birkenhead* and the death and bravery of her soldiers. From the lighthouse the wave is clearly visible but the sound of its crashing on the rock is lost in the distance. Bewitched by its bass and melancholy call, I returned to the tall white tower on a windy and rainy day after

IN MEMORY OF HEROIC EVENT: A plaque designed by Mr. Brian Mansergh, M.I.A., to the commission of the Navy League of South Africa, and struck by the Royal Mint. It is exhibited at the Western Province Pavilion of the Empire Exhibition by courtesy of Lieutenant-Colonel Puntis, president of the League. The plaque will be erected in the wall of the light-house at Danger Point, near Hermanus, off which point the Birkenhead was wrecked.

Plaque before being fitted on to lighthouse, with permission from the Africana Museum

the salvage had closed. It seemed to beckon me to come and share its lonely vigil. Standing next to the lighthouse and oblivious of the rain, I looked down at the savagely fluted plates of rock that form the jagged terrace of Danger Point. The roar of the sea smashing on the rocks, the howl of the north-wester and the dolorous cry of the tower joined in a profound lament.

Rapt in memory, I stood there and gazed out to sea. Inner vision, unfettered by time or weather, telescoped through the sheeting rain and I watched the troopship as it hit the secret rock, heard again the grinding crash of the impact and witnessed the drama and tragedy that followed. I saw the awful drownings of Captain Salmond, Lieutenant-Colonel Seton, Master Brodie, Ensign Russell and the hundreds of soldiers. I saw the three little boats begin their sad journey to shore, with the cries and screams of dying men loud in their ears. I saw the *Lioness* as she reached the cutters and stared at her schooner sails billowing in the wind as she made for the rock and the men clinging to the protruding mainmast.

On the beaches on both sides of the point thick kelp still guards access to land. Just a stone's throw away, Cornet Bond struggled through, pushing aside the long tubular stalks with their brown leafy heads.

The spirit of the *Birkenhead* men will live forever on that bleak and rocky coast. The little towns of Gansbaai and Stanford will continue to boast of their bonds with courage. Our work on the shattered remnants of the wreck will become part of this history too.

Therein lies our great privilege.

A George III sixpence and a Victoria threepenny bit

Obverse of William IV and Victoria threepenny bits and a George III sixpence

Silver half-crowns and gold sovereigns

Silver and gold coins

*Reverse of sovereigns
coated with
conglomerate*

*Reverse of William IV
and Victoria
threepenny bits and a
George III sixpence*

Gold sovereigns

Gold sovereigns in conglomerate

Gold sovereigns and a Victoria half-sovereign. The William IV (bottom left)
was cleaned by brief immersion in 10 per cent citric acid

Reverse of coins shown above

Birkenhead Anecdotes

There are many interesting tales about the *Birkenhead,* which add to the fascination and the mystery. Most are simply legends that have improved with the telling and time.

The tale of the treasure chest that washed up on the beach near Danger Point has many versions. One relates how a poor fisherman from Gansbaai suddenly became very rich soon after the shipwreck. Although no one could prove it, everyone knew that he had found 'the gold'. Another tells how the chest was buried in the sand near the shore, only to be lost again because they had 'forgotten to mark the site'.

There is an aged resident in Gansbaai today who claims to have seen the site where the treasure was buried when he was just a boy, but has never had the time to dig it up. Busy folk, those people of Gansbaai!

Leaning on his elbows at his counter, the barman at the Seaview Hotel told me another tale. 'You see,' he began, 'there was this chap who found the gold in a box from the ship. It was lying in the water by the beach, just there by Kleinbaai. It was very heavy, so he got a couple of guys to help him move it. But he was a crafty one, you know, so he made them all drunk like fowls with his home-made stuff. Then he and this coloured chap hid the box up the beach. When everybody was sober again, there was this amazing fuss, but he made out like he was also asleep, so they couldn't accuse him. I think he ran away overseas afterwards.'

According to another story, Nicholas Dekker, the diver who worked with Tromp van Diggelen, found the gold while diving and retired to France a wealthy man. While we were diving at the *Birkenhead* we asked him if it was true. A wry smile appeared on his creased and weather-beaten face. 'No,' he said, 'I found some sheave blocks and a few other things but gold, no.' Legends die hard, however, and the story of Nicholas Dekker, who lives on a hill just a few kilometres from Stanford, and the *Birkenhead* gold persists.

We spent quite a few evenings at Nicholas Dekker's home. On one

129

occasion he showed us a beautifully decorated chest with intricate floral paintwork never immersed in the sea and complete with a false keyhole to foil would-be thieves. It dates back to the seventeenth century and is currently used for keeping special wines. When Nicholas brought the chest home, the eagle eye of the local gossip spotted him.

'What have you got there?' he asked.

'The *Birkenhead* gold,' said Nicholas.

Gold, shipwrecks and treasure – the stuff that myths and fantasies are made of. Could a chest full of gold be washed ashore? Could 120 boxes of specie, weighing between 3 000 and 5 000 kilograms be washed ashore? But the legends live on.

I heard a story recently about the sharks that attacked the men while they were struggling in the water. 'Did you know,' I was asked, 'that it wasn't sharks that killed the people?'

'No,' I replied, 'what was it?'

'Red steenbras, they were the fish that did it.'

The red steenbras *(Dentex rupestris)* is a southern African fish resembling a snapper. It has a large mouth and sharp savagely pointed teeth and can weigh as much as 25 kilograms. They are a rare catch today and, comparing one to the 1 000-kilogram terror of a great white shark, my mind boggled at the thought of hundreds of steenbras in a feeding frenzy.

'That's very interesting,' I said.

In her delightful book, *Village of the Sea*, published by Human and Rousseau in 1980, Arderne Tredgold describes the history of Hermanus and its people. A whole chapter is devoted to the *Birkenhead* and the stories relating to the drama. She describes how a Mr Stark dived to the wreck and found an octopus the size of a wagon wheel guarding the site. Eluding its clutches, he recovered an old rusted pistol which he later showed to his interpreter, Mr John McGregor Moore of Stanford. Waving the pistol about, he managed to shoot Mr Moore through the arm.

The pistols we had found were in a much more sorry condition, lacking their barrels and most of their workings. They certainly had no dry gunpowder or intact percussion caps. We did see a few octopuses, however. One, about 2 cm in size, was in Grant's condenser and the other was hiding in a cannon. The big octopus is deceased.

The horses of the *Birkenhead* have a story too. In her book Miss Tredgold continues:

'A fisherman had just cast out his line near a place now called Die Stal, when he thought he heard the whinnying of a horse. He left his line and went to investigate. In a gully nearby he saw that three horses were trapped and the only way they could have got into the gully was from the sea.

'With some difficulty he got them all out and took them to Stanford. Here they were received with delight by the survivors from the *Birkenhead*, so much so that the fisherman was given a cheque for £100. In the circumstances it could hardly have come from Captain Wright.

'The fisherman was a simple soul and knew nothing of cheques. He took the piece of paper home and threw it to one side in his cottage. Years later a friend found it there and said:

'What's this cheque doing here?'

'That piece of paper?' said the fisherman. 'The English soldiers from the *Birkenhead* gave it to me when I found some of their horses.'

'That piece of paper was worth £100,' his friend said, 'but it's no use now, it is much too old.''

Appendix

HMS *BIRKENHEAD* ARTEFACT REGISTER IN GRID SEQUENCE

GRID REF.	NO.	DESCRIPTION	DATE
All areas	819	Bronze nails	25/4/88
C3	35	Earthenware jar shard	5/2/86
C3	36	Earthenware jar shard	5/2/86
C3	75	Lead counterweight	14/2/86
C3	595	Gimbal-mounted candle lamp	7/4/88
C3	727	Bell clapper	21/4/88
C3	740	Engraved brass lid	22/4/88
C3	744	Ground-glass stopper	22/4/88
C3	779	Brass standard base	24/4/88
C4	73	Cast brass pulley	14/2/86
C4	605	Ground-glass stopper (decanter)	11/4/88
C4	606	Teaspoon	11/4/88
C4	607	Tablespoon	11/4/88
C4	608	Rifle parts (five pieces)	11/4/88
C4	638	Crystal glass piece	19/4/88
C4	639	Brass ring handle	19/4/88
C4	641	Round deck light	19/4/88
C4	642	Oilstone	19/4/88
C4	694	Monocle	20/4/88
C4	717	Candlestick	21/4/88
C4	804	Bronze stanchion base plate	25/4/88
C5	440	Toilet bowl shard	23/2/88
C5	698	Wedgwood dish	20/4/88
C5	721	Earthenware bottle	21/4/88
C5	730	Silver spoon in conglomerate	22/4/88
C5	771	Circular porthole with lens	24/4/88
C5	772	Circular porthole with lens	24/4/88
C5	773	Circular porthole with lens	24/4/88
C5	774	Circular porthole (lens broken)	24/4/88

C5	775	Circular porthole (lens missing)	24/4/88
C5	703	Small rectangular ceramic pot	20/4/88
D2	807	Bronze base plate	25/4/88
D3	450	Telescope eyepiece	26/2/88
D3	451	Crystal glass base	27/2/88
D3	477	Sextant components (five pieces)	5/3/88
D3	619	Crystal hexagonal columns (two)	15/4/88
D3	632	White saucer	19/4/88
D3	633	Stoneware cup	19/4/88
D3	640	Chronometer	19/4/88
D3	689	Jar shard (mounted rider motif)	20/4/88
D3	716	Ground-glass decanter stopper	21/4/88
D3	737	Sextant eyepiece	22/4/88
D3	739	Sextant eyepiece	22/4/88
D4	71	Earthenware shard	14/2/86
D4	393	Hairbrush handles (two off)	11/2/88
D4	476	Brass bolt (piece)	5/3/88
D4	822	Glass decanter neck	25/4/88
D5	7	Porthole	4/2/86
D5	453	Brass ornament	27/2/88
D5	460	Silver-plated letter opener	29/2/88
D5	470	Musket balls	5/3/88
D5	776	Circular porthole (lens missing)	24/4/88
D5	777	Circular porthole (lens missing)	24/4/88
E3	321	Washbowl shards (ten pieces)	22/5/87
E3	455	Parallel rule	28/2/88
E3	690	Glass ink-well	20/4/88
E3	722	Ground-glass decanter stopper	21/4/88
E3	764	Brass inclinometer	24/4/88
E3	805	Toilet bowl and pump mechanism	25/4/88
E4,4	17	Brass toilet bowl	5/2/86
E4,4	137	Brass valve	17/2/86
E4	715	Silver utensil handle	21/4/88
E4,8	159	Knife handles (four)	19/2/86
E4,8	162	Bottle with ground-glass stopper	19/2/86
E4,8	172	Glass stoppers (two)	19/2/86
E4,9	129	Leather shot pouch	17/2/86
E4,9	130	Rifle parts	17/2/86
E4,9	131	Rifle parts	17/2/86
E4,9	134	Sword scabbard	17/2/86
E4,9	140	Bowl shard (anchor) 'Flora B&T'	17/2/86
E4,9	142	Gent's leather shoe	19/2/86

E4,9	143	Lady's leather shoe	19/2/86
E4,9	150	Hairbrush handle	19/2/86
E4,9	153	Copper birdshot pouch	19/2/86
E4,9	155	Brass hasp	19/2/86
E4,9	156	Brass hasp and staple	19/2/86
E4,9	157	Brass weight	19/2/86
E4,9	219	Percussion cap dispenser	12/3/86
E4,9	144	Shoe fragments	19/2/86
E5,2	154	Crystal container	19/2/86
E5,2	163	Silver spoon	19/2/86
E5,2	165	Silver spoon	19/2/86
E5,2	166	Brass spoon	19/2/86
E5,2	169	Silver pot (two pieces)	19/2/86
E5,2	174	Buttons (five)	19/2/86
E5,2	164	Silver spoon	19/2/86
E5,3	141	Gent's leather shoe	19/2/86
E5,3	146	Leather harness, buckles, clips	19/2/86
E5,3	148	Implement handle	19/2/86
E5,3	149	Implement handle	19/2/86
E5,3	158	Cutthroat razor	19/2/86
E5,3	160	Earthenware lid	19/2/86
E5,3	167	Silver spoon	19/2/86
E5,3	171	Brass tie-rail	19/2/86
E5,3	145	Shoe	19/2/86
E5,3	161	Shard	19/2/86
E5,3	168	Brass belaying pin	19/2/86
E5	475	Porthole pieces	5/3/88
E5,6	6	Steel plate with rivets	4/2/86
E6	478	Brass porthole flap hinge	5/3/88
E6	479	Brass porthole flap hinge (piece)	5/3/88
E6	701	Bone brush handle	20/4/88
E6	750	Silver spoon	23/4/88
E7	813	Complete ventilator flap assembly	25/4/88
F3	4	Brass stanchion	3/2/86
F3	5	Brass balustrade post	3/2/86
F3	332	Inclinometer piece	24/5/87
F3	343	Sword handle	24/5/87
F3	345	'A. Seton' engraved name-plate	24/5/87
F3	432	Glass ink-well	20/2/88
F3	681	Agate handle	20/4/88
F3	685	Copper shot pouch	20/4/88
F3	696	Brass telescope 'Wm. Ashmore London'	20/4/88

134

F3	723	Ground-glass jar lid	21/4/88
F3	732	Gold-plated sword handle	22/4/88
F3	709	Glass bottle seal 'Vieux Cognac'	21/4/88
F4,6	46	Square ink bottle	6/2/86
F4,7	15	Brass catch	5/2/86
F4,7	76	Earthenware jar shard	14/2/86
F4,7	77	Earthenware jar lid shard	14/2/86
F4,7	78	Plate shard	14/2/86
F4,7	121	Crystal glass (crown/anchor)	17/2/86
F4,7	122	Crystal glass (crown/anchor)	17/2/86
F4,7	126	Glass knob	17/2/86
F4,7	147	Implement handle	19/2/86
F4	752	Silver fork	23/4/88
F4	781	Silver tray	24/4/88
F4,8	1	Copper nail	31/1/86
F4,8	39	Washbowl shard	5/2/86
F4,8	123	Porcelain saucer	17/2/86
F4,8	124	Plate	17/2/86
F4,8	152	Wooden rail	19/2/86
F4,8	125	Lid	17/2/86
F4,9	32	Shard (broad arrow)	5/2/86
F4,9	33	Shard	5/2/86
F4,9	34	Shard	5/2/86
F5,1	68	Earthenware jar lid	14/2/86
F5,1	69	Earthenware jar shard	14/2/86
F5,1	70	Earthenware jar shard	14/2/86
F5,1	72	Earthenware jar lid shard	14/2/86
F5,1	79	Glass lens shard	14/2/86
F5,1	139	Brass keyhole cover	17/2/86
F5,1	138	Brass doorknob	17/2/86
F5,2	66	Washbowl shard	14/2/86
F5,2	67	Washbowl shard	14/2/86
F5,2	80	Cup shard	14/2/86
F5,2	88	Musket ball	14/2/86
F5,2	173	Glass bottle with stopper	19/2/86
F5,3	2	Wooden sheave	31/1/86
F5,3	40	Washbowl shard	5/2/86
F5,3	41	Jug shard (Powell Potter, Bristol)	5/2/86
F5,3	43	Glass bottle fragment	5/2/86
F5,3	57	Earthenware jar neck	8/2/86
F5,3	89	Bottle	14/2/86
F5,3	91	Bone brush handle	14/2/86

F5,4	94	Earthenware jug	15/2/86
F5,4	95	Night-lamp jug (Doulton)	16/2/86
F5,4	96	Porcelain lid for no. 53	16/2/86
F5,4	98	Brass lock plate	16/2/86
F5,4	99	Silver spoon	16/2/86
F5,4	100	Silver sugar tongs	16/2/86
F5,4	101	Plate shard (anchor)	16/2/86
F5,4	102	Jug shard (Doulton: dogs in relief)	16/2/86
F5,4	103	Brass pulley	16/2/86
F5,4	104	Cupboard handle	16/2/86
F5,4	105	Bell clapper	16/2/86
F5,4	106	Brass lamp part	16/2/86
F5,4	107	Staff end	16/2/86
F5,4	108	Brass buckle	16/2/86
F5,4	109	Pewter spoon	16/2/86
F5,4	110	Silver spoon	16/2/86
F5,4	111	Silver spoon	16/2/86
F5,4	112	Silver spoon	16/2/86
F5,4	113	Silver spoon	16/2/86
F5,4	114	Silver spoon	16/2/86
F5,4	115	Brass badge (triangular)	16/2/86
F5,4	116	Silver spoon	16/2/86
F5,4	117	Ornament	16/2/86
F5,4	118	Earthenware jar lid	16/2/86
F5,4	119	Brass catch	16/2/86
F5,4	127	Jug shard (Doulton)	17/2/86
F5,4	128	Jug shard (Doulton)	17/2/86
F5,4	132	Conglomerated porcelain	17/2/86
F5,4	170	Brass pulley	19/2/86
F5,4	97	Brass hinge strap	16/2/86
F5	426	Copper tag 'Steerage star. no. 2'	18/2/88
F5	428	Sword handle	18/2/88
F5	457	Silver spoon	28/2/88
F5,5	20	Button (12th Lancers)	6/2/86
F5,5	30	Bottle neck	5/2/86
F5,5	31	Bottle neck	5/2/86
F5,5	55	Glass bottle base	7/2/86
F5,5	81	Brass hasp	14/2/86
F5,5	82	Brass hinge part	14/2/86
F5,5	83	Brass gimbal lamp	14/2/86
F5,5	85	Knife handle	14/2/86
F5,5	86	Bottle neck	14/2/86

F5,5	87	Bottle neck	14/2/86
F5,5	90	Brass eye	14/2/86
F5,5	93	Pewter teapot stand	15/2/86
F5,5	92	Pewter spoon	15/2/86
F5,6	62	Earthenware jar lid	8/2/86
F5	758	Candleholder dish	23/4/88
F5	783	Pewter bowl	24/4/88
F5,9	133	Mallet head	17/2/86
F6	198	White china plate	8/3/86
F6	199	White china plate	8/3/86
F6	228	Brass grid	14/3/86
F6	458	Round porthole	29/2/88
F6	459	Porthole flap hinge	29/2/88
F6	472	Brass mortise lock	5/3/88
F6	778	Rectangular brass vent grid	24/4/88
F7	249	Plate shard	3/4/86
F7	250	White china plate	3/4/86
F7	436	Silver forks (three pieces)	22/2/88
F7	437	Bowl shard	22/2/88
F7	441	Grapeshot canister end and shot	23/2/88
F7	471	Earthenware jar & bottle	5/3/88
F7	474	Sword scabbard piece	5/3/88
F7	806	Rectangular bronze grid	25/4/88
F7	814	Complete ventilator flap assembly	25/4/88
G3	329	Knife handle	24/5/87
G3	337	Brass post	24/5/87
G3	338	Brass post	24/5/87
G3	688	Copper handle (lion's head)	20/4/88
G4	330	Fork handle (?)	24/5/87
G5,1	16	Wooden sheave	5/2/86
G5,1	37	Bottle fragment	5/2/86
G5,1	120	Wooden mast block	16/2/86
G5,2	23	Brass ornament (thistle motif)	6/2/86
G5,2	27	Copper jug (three pieces)	8/2/86
G5,2	42	Bowl shard	5/2/86
G5,2	47	New japan stone plate shard (anchor)	6/2/86
G5,2	48	Brass turnbuckle	6/2/86
G5,4	25	Metal lid	8/2/86
G5,4	26	Silver teaspoon (broad arrow)	8/2/86
G5,4	28	Crystal decanter	8/2/86
G5,4	29	Wooden handle	8/2/86
G5,4	38	Crystal tumbler base (C.P.)	5/2/86

G5,4	45	Crystal tumbler base (C.P.)	6/2/86
G5,4	49	Earthenware jar shard (Powell Potter)	6/2/86
G5,4	50	Earthenware jar shard (Powell Potter)	7/2/86
G5,4	51	Earthenware jar shard (Powell Potter)	7/2/86
G5,4	52	Earthenware jar lid (Powell Potter)	7/2/86
G5,4	53	Rectangular porcelain dish	7/2/86
G5,4	54	Glass bottle base	7/2/86
G5,4	56	Glass bottle base	7/2/86
G5,4	58	Plate shard	8/2/86
G5,4	59	Bottle neck	8/2/86
G5,4	60	Bottle neck	8/2/86
G5,4	61	Earthenware jar complete	8/2/86
G5,4	63	Plate shard (thistle)	8/2/86
G5,4	64	Crystal glass shard	8/2/86
G5,4	65	Teapot shard	8/2/86
G5,4	151	Wooden handle	19/2/86
G5,4	175	Earthenware jug	19/2/86
G5	427	Crystal glass base	18/2/88
G5	429	Brush back (bone)	18/2/88
G5	435	Earthenware jar lid	20/2/88
G5	448	Cast ornamental piece	26/2/88
G5	449	Silver teaspoon	26/2/88
G5,5	8	Syringe	5/2/86
G5,5	21	Brass 'T' piece	6/2/86
G5,5	22	Brass ornament	6/2/86
G5,5	24	Brass skylight frame	6/2/86
G5,5	74	Gimbal bracket	14/2/86
G5,5	84	Copper oil can	14/2/86
G5,5	257	Compass pieces	6/4/86
G5,5	258	Brass hinge pieces (two off)	6/4/86
G5,5	259	Octagonal brass sleeve	6/4/86
G5,6	9	Letter opener	5/2/86
G5,6	10	Brass hasp	5/2/86
G5,6	11	Brass hasp	5/2/86
G5,6	12	Musket ball mould	5/2/86
G5,7	135	Brass ring with three legs	17/2/86
G5,7	136	Brass lamp bracket	17/2/86
G5	728	Glass stopper	22/4/88
G5,8	19	Compass gimbal assembly	5/2/86
G5,8	44	Blue/white porcelain shard	5/2/86
G5	823	Broken bottle	25/4/88
G5,9	13	Brass button	5/2/86

G7	434	Brass badge '91'	20/2/88
G7	443	Brass buckle (medal hanger)	23/2/88
G7	469	Copper key-tag 'Purser's Steward'	5/3/88
G7	473	Wine bottle	5/3/88
G7	754	Brown glass bottle	23/4/88
G7	784	Leather shoe sole	24/4/88
G7	785	Leather shoe sole	24/4/88
G7	786	Leather shoe sole	24/4/88
G7	815	Ventilator frames & hinges (three pieces)	25/4/88
G7	726	Shaving brush handle	21/4/88
G8	196	Pistol	8/3/86
G8	241	Bottle base	27/3/86
G8	242	Bottle base	27/3/86
G8	243	Bottle base	27/3/86
G8	244	Bottle base	27/3/86
G8	618	Spirit bottle	15/4/88
H3	344	'R.S.Bond' engraved nameplate	24/5/87
H3	692	Gold fob watch back	20/4/88
H3	724	Gold-plated sword handle guard	21/4/88
H3	733	Powder measure	22/4/88
H3	734	Brass container with two hinged lids	22/4/88
H4	741	Gold-plated sword handle guard	22/4/88
H5	18	Copper handle	5/2/86
H5	416	Brass bell	18/2/88
H5	417	Copper lid	18/2/88
H5	418	Bottle neck	18/2/88
H5	419	Bottle neck	18/2/88
H5	420	Bottle neck	18/2/88
H5	421	Bottle neck	18/2/88
H5	422	Bottle neck	18/2/88
H5	423	Bottle neck	18/2/88
H5	424	Bottle base	18/2/88
H5	425	Bottle neck	18/2/88
H6	430	Brass lock pieces	18/2/88
H6	431	Wooden peg	20/2/88
H6	438	Glazed hand-painted lid	22/2/88
H6	439	Plate shard	22/2/88
H6	447	Brass arm	26/2/88
H7	177	Shoes (two)	28/2/86
H7	178	Shoe	28/2/86
H7	179	Wine bottle	28/2/86
H7	386	Wooden telescope pieces	10/2/88

H7	388	Shaving brush bowl piece (ref 381)	10/2/88
H7	403	Crystal wine glass piece	13/2/88
H7	454	Copper bell?	27/2/88
H7	711	Bottle base 'Powell & Co. Bristol'	21/4/88
H7	760	Broken bottle	24/4/88
H7	762	Clear green bottle (broken)	24/4/88
H7	763	Clear green bottle (broken)	24/4/88
H8	394	Bottle tops (two off)	11/2/88
H8	401	Bottle neck	13/2/88
H8	402	Bottle neck	13/2/88
H8	615	Set of door furniture	15/4/88
H8	745	Rectangular bottle base	22/4/88
H8	746	Clear green glass bottle	22/4/88
H8	747	Brown glass bottle	22/4/88
I3	452	Lignum vitae sheave	27/2/88
I3	481	Brass and lignum sheave	8/3/88
I3	482	Brass pulley wheel	8/3/88
I3	751	Glass ink-well in conglomerate	23/4/88
I3	753	Sword handle in conglomerate	23/4/88
I3	761	Wooden drawer front	24/4/88
I3	797	Earthenware ink-well	24/4/88
I3	798	Earthenware ink-well	24/4/88
I3	811	Bronze cowling	25/4/88
I3	816	Ventilator frames & hinges (four pieces)	25/4/88
I4	480	Gold-plated medal (.oit peninsula)	8/3/88
I4	731	Decorative chain chinstrap	22/4/88
I4	748	Sword handle guard	23/4/88
I4	812	Bronze cowling	25/4/88
I5	404	Brass nails (two off)	13/2/88
I5	407	Rifle	14/2/88
I5	411	Wooden armchair armrest	14/2/88
I5	414	Turned wooden piece	14/2/88
I5	415	Shaving brush (see 381, 388)	14/2/88
I5	445	Metal dish	23/2/88
I5	446	Drain fitting	23/2/88
I5	738	Silver fob watch (no back)	22/4/88
I6	3	Bronze sheave	2/2/86
I6	200	Brass rifle butt plate	11/3/86
I6	377	Wooden sheave	4/2/88
I6	378	Wooden sheave	4/2/88
I6	389	Sextant eyepiece	11/2/88
I6	405	Plate	13/2/88

I6	408	Mallet head	14/2/88
I6	409	Wooden disc	14/2/88
I6	410	Wooden brush back	14/2/88
I6	699	Bottle	20/4/88
I6	700	Rectangular bottle with stopper	20/4/88
I6	725	Copper tag 'Steward Berth'	21/4/88
I6	755	White porcelain saucer	23/4/88
I6	756	Silver fork	23/4/88
I6	757	Bottle neck with stopper	23/4/88
I7	176	Sword scabbard end	24/2/86
I7	346	Leather pouches	19/1/88
I7	351	8 oz. earthenware pot (two pieces)	19/1/88
I7	352	Brass label 'Brown Brothers'	19/1/88
I7	353	Copper tag 'Steerage port no. 6'	19/1/88
I7	385	Wooden mallet head	10/2/88
I7	400	Brass base plate	12/2/88
I7	406	Brush	13/2/88
I7	412	Leather pouch	14/2/88
I7	413	Leather belt	14/2/88
I8	349	Pistol	19/1/88
I8	371	Leather sole	3/2/88
I8	376	Rowlock	4/2/88
I8	387	Leather pouch	10/2/88
I8	392	Brass belt buckles and clip	11/2/88
I8	598	Spoon	10/4/88
I8	599	Spoon	10/4/88
I8	600	Bone knife handles (two pieces)	10/4/88
I8	601	Spoon	10/4/88
I8	602	Bone knife handle	10/4/88
I8	614	Crystal bowl piece	15/4/88
I9	817	Bronze sheave	25/4/88
J4	326	Brass rifle butt plate	23/5/87
J4	327	Brass knob	23/5/87
J4	382	Sword handle piece	3/2/88
J4	390	Brass mortise lock	11/2/88
J4	442	Ramrod handle	23/2/88
J5	322	Jar lid	22/5/87
J5	323	Silver fork	23/5/87
J5	324	Brass oarlock	23/5/87
J5	325	Glazed goblet	23/5/87
J5	333	Skylight prism	24/5/87
J5	334	Skylight prism	24/5/87

J5	354	Earthenware ink-well	19/1/88
J5	379	Lid 'Rimmel's genuine bear grease'	4/2/88
J5	380	Glass bottle seal VR	3/2/88
J5	683	Shoulder decorations	20/4/88
J5	684	Pocket compass	20/4/88
J5	713	Bone brush handle	21/4/88
J5	824	Flute section	25/4/88
J6	181	Brass oil lamp	1/3/86
J6	182	Brass oil lamp part	1/3/86
J6	183	Brass hinge	1/3/86
J6	185	Brass butterfly clamp	1/3/86
J6	186	Brass lock	1/3/86
J6	187	Brass cupboard handle	1/3/86
J6	188	Brass key	1/3/86
J6	189	Brass nut and bolt	1/3/86
J6	191	Brass hasp piece	1/3/86
J6	197	Brass bearing cap	8/3/86
J6	216	Brass gimbal	12/3/86
J6	217	Brass burner ring	12/3/86
J6	230	Shoehorn	20/3/86
J6	348	Wooden syringe	19/1/88
J6	712	Glass bottle seal 'John McKenna'	21/4/88
J6	759	Broken earthenware jar	24/4/88
J7	180	Navy uniform pieces with buttons	1/3/86
J7	184	Brass gun calibre gauge	1/3/86
J7	190	Silver spoon	1/3/86
J7	193	Pistol	7/3/86
J7	194	Child's shoe sole	8/3/86
J7	195	Earthenware bottle	8/3/86
J7	222	Glass tube	14/3/86
J7	226	Brass nameplate 'G.A.Lucas Esq.'	14/3/86
J7	236	Sword scabbard end	22/3/86
J7	237	Silver fork	22/3/86
J7	238	Brass door catch	22/3/86
J7	239	Brass ornamental piece	22/3/86
J7	240	Copper handle	22/3/86
J7	245	Bottle base	27/3/86
J7	246	Tumbler base	2/4/86
J7	251	Earthenware shard	3/4/86
J7	252	Earthenware shard	3/4/86
J7	253	China plate shard	3/4/86
J7	254	Earthenware lid	3/4/86

J7	255	Glazed handle	3/4/86
J7	256	Plate shard	3/4/86
J7	355	Braided wooden balls (two off)	19/1/88
J7	356	Brass doorknob	19/1/88
J7	693	6 oz. earthenware jar	20/4/88
J7	718	Stoneware jar	21/4/88
J7	719	Stoneware jar lid	21/4/88
J7	720	Stoneware jar lid	21/4/88
J7	729	Pair of children's stirrups	22/4/88
J8	358	Leather shoe pieces and sock	20/1/88
J8	374	Brass oil lamp base	3/2/88
J8	384	Pulley block (wooden)	10/2/88
J8	396	Brass door-keep	12/2/88
J8	397	Brass lock plate	12/2/88
J8	398	Lead plate (six pounds)	12/2/88
J8	399	Lead plate (five pounds)	12/2/88
J8	433	Brass tape measure	20/2/88
J8	596	Rifle cleaning rod	10/4/88
J8	597	Oilstone	10/4/88
J8	603	Brass chain	10/4/88
J8	604	Drawer handle	10/4/88
J8	825	Small bearing	25/4/88
J9	695	Copper tag 'Signal Door'	20/4/88
J9	799	Brass pulley	24/4/88
K4	341	Brass lock and doorknob	24/5/87
K4	342	Brush handles (two)	24/5/87
K5	335	Brush handle	24/5/87
K5	336	Brass hinge	24/5/87
K5	339	Brass ring assembly	24/5/87
K5	340	Skylight prism	24/5/87
K5	350	Blue/white shards (four pieces) jug	19/1/88
K5	381	Shaving brush top (see 388, 415)	3/2/88
K5	444	Brass end plug (artillery?)	23/2/88
K5	800	Shaving brush in conglomerate	24/4/88
K6	347	Shaving brush/bowl	19/1/88
K6	359	Silver spoon	20/1/88
K6	360	Brass lock plate	20/1/88
K6	363	Hinge piece (John Jones 6 Regent St)	26/1/88
K6	364	Bronze base plate	26/1/88
K6	365	Wooden pulleys (two off)	26/1/88
K6	366	Wooden hairbrush back	26/1/88
K6	368	Bone knife handle	26/1/88

K6	369	Plate shard '. . . and Garrett'	26/1/88
K6	391	Signal gun shot	11/2/88
K6	456	Hip-flask	28/2/88
K6	621	Square bottle	18/4/88
K6	622	Medicine bottle	18/4/88
K6	623	Medicine bottle	18/4/88
K6	624	Medicine bottle	18/4/88
K6	625	Medicine measure	18/4/88
K6	626	Medicine bottle	18/4/88
K6	627	Pocket watch	18/4/88
K6	679	Mercury bottle	20/4/88
K6	680	Rectangular cut-glass container	20/4/88
K6	682	Rectangular bottle with stopper	20/4/88
K6	691	Pewter syringe	20/4/88
K6	705	Medicine bottle	21/4/88
K6	714	Thermometer indicator plate	21/4/88
K7	201	Brass fire-hose coupling	11/3/86
K7	202	Brass fire-hose coupling	11/3/86
K7	203	Brass coupling	11/3/86
K7	204	Brass coupling	11/3/86
K7	229	Pipe bowl	20/3/86
K7	231	Metal bowl	20/3/86
K7	232	Brass face plate	21/3/86
K7	247	Brass catch	2/4/86
K7	357	Wooden peg	19/1/88
K7	361	Bronze bearing (complete)	23/1/88
K7	362	Bronze bearing (half)	23/1/88
K7	367	Brass wing nut	26/1/88
K7	372	Brass spindle bracket	3/2/88
K7	373	Brass pulley block	3/2/88
K7	395	Brass bearing cap	12/2/88
K7	801	Folding knife	24/4/88
K8	192	Brass valve	7/3/86
K8	233	Brass rope thimbles	21/3/86
K8	234	Brass pulley	21/3/86
K8	235	Brass fire-hose connector	22/3/86
K8	383	Pistol	10/2/88
K9	643	Brass valve	19/4/88
K9	780	Oil drip pot	24/4/88
K9	827	Small bollard	25/4/88
L5	328	Musket ball mould	23/5/87
L5	370	Brass relief valve	26/1/88

L6	749	Bottle with ground-glass stopper	23/4/88
L7	227	Brass valve	14/3/86
M4	331	Lead compass housing	24/5/87
M5	802	Bollard with slotted grid	25/4/88
M5	803	Large bollard	25/4/88
M5	826	Small lead sounding weight	25/4/88
N9	14	Brass valve	5/2/86
N10	611	Brass valve	13/4/88
N10	612	Brass pulleys (four pieces)	13/4/88
N10	613	Brass pulleys (two pieces)	13/4/88
N10	617	Brass clamp	15/4/88
N11	375	Brass harness buckle	3/2/88
N11	465	Silver spoon	5/3/88
N11	466	Bone brush handle	5/3/88
O11	313	Copper pipe	9/5/87
O11	467	Glass deck light	5/3/88
O11	468	Bone knife handle	5/3/88
O12	289	Dead-eye	10/4/87
O12	303	Fire-hose connector	29/4/87
O12	312	Conglomerated bowl (two pieces)	9/5/87
O12	810	Bronze frame with round skylight	25/4/88
O12	821	Bronze sheave	25/4/88
O13	265	Gear-shift base plate	14/2/87
O13	268	Lead flange gasket	1/3/87
O13	273	Deck skylight lens and frame	18/3/87
O13	288	Plate in conglomerate	10/4/87
O14	274	Wooden pulley	24/3/87
O14	275	Wooden pulley	24/3/87
P12	280	Bottle base (Ricketts Bristol)	29/3/87
P12	281	Porthole frame	3/4/87
P12	285	Earthenware jar lid	8/4/87
P12	318	Cold cream jar lid	22/5/87
P12	319	Plate shard	22/5/87
P13	266	Rudder pintle	27/2/87
P13	267	Rudder pintle	27/2/87
P13	706	Bottle of chilis 'Lea & Perrins'	21/4/88
P13	707	Bottle, octagonal base	21/4/88
P13	708	Bottle, clear green glass	21/4/88
Q12	293	Bottle, 'Lea & Perrins'	17/4/87
Q13	290	Conglomerated musket balls	12/4/87
Q14	291	Hairbrush backs (two off)	12/4/87
Q14	292	Brass pipe union	12/4/87

Q14	294	Mace headpiece	17/4/87
Q14	295	Brass rail bracket	17/4/87
Q14	297	Brass buckles	19/4/87
Q14	298	Brass rail bracket	25/4/87
Q14	301	Gear-shift base plate	29/4/87
Q14	302	Oil drip cup	29/4/87
Q16	818	Bronze control plate	25/4/88
R8	308	Copper stack with cowling	3/5/87
R8	309	Brass cowling	5/5/87
R8	310	Conglomerated bottle base	9/5/87
R8	792	Musket balls (21 pieces)	24/4/88
R9	205	Brass ring with handles	11/3/86
R9	206	Brass pot handle	11/3/86
R9	207	Brass rifle side-plate	11/3/86
R9	208	Brass tap	11/3/86
R9	209	Brass rifle trigger guard	11/3/86
R9	210	Brass ornamental headpiece	11/3/86
R9	212	Brass hemisphere	11/3/86
R10	271	Brass oil funnel	11/3/87
R10	272	Double wooden pulley	11/3/87
R11	270	Copper pot lid	5/3/87
R11	282	Pewter box	6/4/87
R11	306	Crucible	3/5/87
R11	311	Oil lamp pieces	9/5/87
R11	782	Pewter container corner piece	24/4/88
S4	296	Brass pulleys (two off)	19/4/87
S4	299	Brass pulley	25/4/87
S7	316	Copper container with valve	19/5/87
S8	260	Galley stove top plate	29/1/87
S8	261	Bin hinge	29/1/87
S8	262	Coal scuttle	6/2/87
S8	263	Brass valve	8/2/87
S8	264	Pipe fittings & stopper	8/2/87
S8	283	Copper pot lid	6/4/87
S8	284	Brass porthole frame hinge	6/4/87
S8	286	Copper stove cover plate	8/4/87
S8	287	Gimbal bracket	8/4/87
S8	300	Jelly mould	25/4/87
S9	269	Copper pot lid	1/3/87
S9	307	(Copper?) cover	3/5/87
S11	276	Shaving brush cup	24/3/87
S11	277	Brass door-latch	27/3/87

S11	279	Medicine bottle	29/3/87
S16	616	Wooden sheaves (four pieces)	15/4/88
S16	634	Copper tag 'Fore hold port'	19/4/88
S18	765	Round skylight lens	24/4/88
S18	766	Round skylight lens with frame	24/4/88
T5	214	Glass skylight lens	11/3/86
T5	320	Red glass fragment	22/5/87
T9	248	Flap valve	3/4/86
U8	221	Brass rail	12/3/86
U9	211	Brass railing end-piece	11/3/86
U9	213	Glass stopper	11/3/86
U12	462	Brass padlock	4/3/88
U12	463	Brass gun butt piece	4/3/88
U12	620	Earthenware jar full of percussion caps	16/4/88
U12	461	Earthenware ink-well	4/3/88
U13	278	Brass bell crown piece	29/3/87
U13	677	Crown piece of ship's bell	20/4/88
V8	218	Brass buckles (ten pieces)	12/3/86
V9	215	Gold pendant clasp	11/3/86
V9	220	Circular glass skylight lens	12/3/86
V9	223	Brass hook	14/3/86
V9	224	Buttons	14/3/86
V9	225	Brass buckles and clips	14/3/86
V11	464	Brass buckles (13 pieces)	4/3/88
V11	637	Brass hasp	19/4/88
V11	820	Skylight frame and lens	25/4/88
V12	702	Crucifix	20/4/88
V12	742	Clay pipe bowl	22/4/88
V12	743	Brass container with screw-on lid	22/4/88
V12	808	Bronze fairlead	25/4/88
V14	317	Copper stanchion	22/5/87
W12	594	Rubberised overshoe	5/4/88
W12	609	Bone knife handle '73' 2396?	13/4/88
W12	610	Bone knife handle	13/4/88
W12	635	Pocket knife	19/4/88
W12	697	Wooden brush handle	20/4/88
W12	704	Pewter syringe	21/4/88
W12	710	Pewter syringe	21/4/88
W12	809	Bronze fairlead	25/4/88
W13	628	Regimental buttons (six pieces)	18/4/88
W13	629	Regimental emblems (12 pieces)	18/4/88
W13	630	Regimental buckle	18/4/88

W13	631	Regimental badges 74th (three pieces)	18/4/88
W13	678	Pewter syringe	20/4/88
W13	770	Brass pulley block	24/4/88
X12	483	Bone brush handles (six pieces)	27/3/88
X12	484	Brush 2564	27/3/88
X12	485	Brush 73rd 2485	27/3/88
X12	486	Brush 73rd 2337	27/3/88
X12	487	Brush 73rd 2327	27/3/88
X12	488	Brush 2204	27/3/88
X12	489	Brush 6th Foot 2124	27/3/88
X12	490	Brush 2721	27/3/88
X12	491	Brush C2743 & C2726	27/3/88
X12	492	Brush 73rd 2780	27/3/88
X12	493	Brush 74th 3125 E. Mc L.	27/3/88
X12	494	Brush 3296	27/3/88
X12	495	Brush B2676	27/3/88
X12	496	Brush 1881	27/3/88
X12	497	Brush 74th D3195 A.B.	27/3/88
X12	498	Brush 73rd 2305L	27/3/88
X12	499	Brush W.B.	27/3/88
X12	500	Brush 1066 S. Latham	27/3/88
X12	501	Brush JT Lnry	27/3/88
X12	502	Brush J. Harper	27/3/88
X12	503	Brush J. Deans	27/3/88
X12	504	Brush D.J.M.	28/3/88
X12	505	Brush J.G. Wisn	28/3/88
X12	506	Brush 91st J. Drury No. 4	28/3/88
X12	507	Brush 74th .I.3183 J.K.	28/3/88
X12	508	Brush 2708	28/3/88
X12	509	Brush 74th .F.3182 J.T.	28/3/88
X12	510	Brush 73rd 2396	28/3/88
X12	511	Brush A2674	28/3/88
X12	512	Brush 73rd 2835	28/3/88
X12	513	Brush 73rd 2812	28/3/88
X12	514	Brush 1438	28/3/88
X12	515	Brush 1489	28/3/88
X12	516	Brush 91st 27.. J. Holden	28/3/88
X12	517	Brush A	28/3/88
X12	518	Brush C2704 (broken)	28/3/88
X12	519	Brush 4th 2698 D. Pratt	28/3/88
X12	520	Wooden shaving brush handle	29/3/88
X12	521	Bone brush handle	29/3/88

X12	522	Bone shaving brushes (three pieces)	29/3/88
X12	523	Shoe-brush 73rd A2165	29/3/88
X12	524	Shoe-brush 91st No. 4 D.P.	29/3/88
X12	525	Shoe-brush 2505	29/3/88
X12	526	Shoe-brush I 3183 J.K.	29/3/88
X12	527	Shoe-brush 2762	29/3/88
X12	528	Shoe-brush 73rd 2396	29/3/88
X12	529	Shoe-brush 1.37 S.H.R.	29/3/88
X12	530	Shoe-brush 2707	29/3/88
X12	531	Shoe-brush 2674	29/3/88
X12	532	Shoe-brush 73rd 2835	29/3/88
X12	533	Shoe-brush .D. 3189 W.S.	29/3/88
X12	534	Shoe-brush 32 .Regt. 73rd. 2812	29/3/88
X12	535	Shoe-brush 2672 J.H.	29/3/88
X12	536	Rifle cleaning brush J. Thompson	1/4/88
X12	537	Rifle cleaning brush (bone as 536)	1/4/88
X12	538	Silver spoon Cavanagh	1/4/88
X12	539	Silver spoon H. 74th 3113 J. Nielson	1/4/88
X12	540	Silver spoon	1/4/88
X12	541	Silver spoon 73rd 2305	1/4/88
X12	542	Bone knife handle 2124	1/4/88
X12	543	Bone knife handle 73rd 2812	1/4/88
X12	544	Bone knife handle A2663	1/4/88
X12	545	Bone knife handle 2701	1/4/88
X12	546	Bone knife handle GR.2788	1/4/88
X12	547	Bone knife handle 2883	1/4/88
X12	548	Bone knife handle 73rd 2780	1/4/88
X12	549	Bone knife handle 73rd 2815	1/4/88
X12	550	Bone knife handle A2705	1/4/88
X12	551	Bone knife handle	1/4/88
X12	552	Bone knife handle	1/4/88
X12	553	Bone knife handle 74th H3113 J. Nielson	1/4/88
X12	554	Bone knife handle 3686	1/4/88
X12	555	Bone knife handle	1/4/88
X12	556	Bone knife handle 73rd ?81	1/4/88
X12	557	Bone knife handle	1/4/88
X12	558	Bone knife handle	1/4/88
X12	559	Bone knife handle	1/4/88
X12	560	Bone knife handle	1/4/88
X12	561	Bone knife handle	1/4/88
X12	562	Bone knife handles (four pieces)	1/4/88
X12	563	1/2 Bone knife handle 74th H3113 J. Nielson	1/4/88

X12	564	1/2 Bone knife handle 73rd 2205	1/4/88
X12	565	1/2 Bone knife handle 1438	1/4/88
X12	566	1/2 Bone knife handle 73rd 2204	1/4/88
X12	567	1/2 Bone knife handle 73rd 2831	1/4/88
X12	568	Clay pipes, seven bowls, three stem pieces	5/4/88
X12	569	Penknife handles, mother-of-pearl	5/4/88
X12	570	Cutthroat handle 73rd 2337	5/4/88
X12	571	Cutthroat handle 73rd 2385	5/4/88
X12	572	Cutthroat handle	5/4/88
X12	573	Cutthroat handle (half-piece)	5/4/88
X12	574	Regimental buttons (46 pieces)	5/4/88
X12	575	Regimental buttons (154 pieces)	5/4/88
X12	576	Brass (webbing) studs (28 pieces)	5/4/88
X12	577	Regimental buttons (262 pieces)	5/4/88
X12	578	Regimental buttons (222 pieces)	5/4/88
X12	579	Webbing buckles (191 pieces)	5/4/88
X12	580	Webbing buckles (200 pieces)	5/4/88
X12	581	Webbing buckles (200 pieces)	5/4/88
X12	582	Webbing buckles (200 pieces)	5/4/88
X12	583	Tassel holders (21 pieces)	5/4/88
X12	584	Brass plate buckles (17 pieces)	5/4/88
X12	585	Regimental buttons (28 pieces)	5/4/88
X12	586	Thistle/Tudor Rose badges (ten pieces)	5/4/88
X12	587	6th Regiment badges (large) (three pieces)	5/4/88
X12	588	12th Regiment badges (large, two pieces)	5/4/88
X12	589	73rd Regiment badges (large) (five pieces)	5/4/88
X12	590	91st Regiment badges (large, two pieces)	5/4/88
X12	591	Shoe polish box	5/4/88
X12	592	Button polishing boards (four pieces)	5/4/88
X12	593	Razor strop board	5/4/88
X12	636	Teaspoon	19/4/88
X12	644	Spoon 73rd 2204	19/4/88
X12	645	Spoon	19/4/88
X12	646	Spoon A2764	19/4/88
X12	647	Spoon 73rd 2835	19/4/88
X12	648	Spoon 73rd 2780	19/4/88
X12	649	Spoon	19/4/88
X12	650	Spoon	19/4/88
X12	651	Spoon 91st W. Dodd	19/4/88
X12	652	Spoon	19/4/88

X12	653	Spoon 74th F3182 J.T.	19/4/88
X12	654	Spoon	19/4/88
X12	655	Spoon	19/4/88
X12	656	Spoon	19/4/88
X12	657	Spoon	19/4/88
X12	658	Spoon	19/4/88
X12	659	Spoon	19/4/88
X12	660	Spoon 73rd 2305	19/4/88
X12	661	Spoon	19/4/88
X12	662	Spoon 91st D.G.	19/4/88
X12	663	Bone brush handle 74th F3150 J.B.	19/4/88
X12	664	Bone brush handle 74th F1539 J.D.	19/4/88
X12	665	Bone brush handle 2693 A.	19/4/88
X12	666	Bone brush handle 2663 A.	19/4/88
X12	667	Bone brush handle 1411	19/4/88
X12	668	Bone brush handle 74th J. Griffeth	19/4/88
X12	669	Shaving brush 3084	19/4/88
X12	670	Knife handle 3296	19/4/88
X12	671	Shaving brush 2698	19/4/88
X12	672	73rd Regiment badge	20/4/88
X12	673	Badge Gibraltar, per mare per terram	20/4/88
X12	674	91st Regiment badge	20/4/88
X12	675	Badge Gibraltar, per mare per terram	20/4/88
X12	676	73rd Regiment badge	20/4/88
X12	735	6th Regiment badge	22/4/88
X12	736	Bone brush handle	22/4/88
X12	787	Regimental buttons (453 pieces)	24/4/88
X12	788	Brass studs (24 pieces)	24/4/88
X12	789	Brass webbing buckles (130 pieces)	24/4/88
X12	790	Regimental buttons (557 pieces)	24/4/88
X12	791	Brass studs (22 pieces)	24/4/88
X12	793	Brass decorative spheres (five pieces)	24/4/88
X12	794	Brass rose decorations (six pieces)	24/4/88
X12	796	Gimbal oil lamp in conglomerate	24/4/88
X12	795	Brass buttons (124 pieces)	24/4/88
Y17	304	Lead line	29/4/87
Y17	305	Lead line	29/4/87
Y17	314	Brass pulley (Handy Billy)	18/5/87
Y17	315	Brass shaft	18/5/87
Y17	767	Small lead sounding weight	24/4/88
Y17	768	Small lead sounding weight	24/4/88
Y17	769	Large lead sounding weight	24/4/88